I thank God
for giving me the perfect wife
to fill every void
and deficiency in my life.
I had not lived until this
gift was given to me.
To my sweetheart Julie,
I love you.
There are still no words!
To my wonderful son Matthew,
what a Joy you are to me.
My life has been richly
blessed with your love.
Grow my Son,
become your own Man.
It is an Honor to be
your Father.
Love Dad

❊ Chapters ❊

Are you the One That Can Take "The Tithing Challenge?"

All you have to do is publicly prove in our presence from scripture, using proper biblical hermeneutics, that tithing 10% is a New Covenant command to be practiced by the church today. We will take it one step further; **IF** you can find anywhere in the Old Testament Law where tithes (as it applied to everyone) were paid in the form of money.

Or, perhaps, you can find One New Testament believer that paid a 10% tithe after the cross of Calvary. Name just one New Testament Saint in scripture from the resurrection of Jesus Christ who paid a 10% tithe? If you can, then put it in the mail and we will send you ***One Hundred*** times the price of this book without a public forum.

One Hundred Times the Price of this Book Without a Public Forum.

Perhaps Your Pastor, Deacon, Elder, Or Church Member Can Take "The Tithing Challenge"

It is time for the church leaders to get honest and truthful with the children of God over the entire issue of tithing. There needs to be a clear foundational and spiritual understanding of our Father's heart and what His real intentions were in the realm of tithing and giving.

Where are the Bereans within your church who can publicly prove in my presence that they have the right to collect tithes from you? Can <u>Benny Hinn</u> do it? ... How about <u>John Hagee?</u> ... Let's not forget heretics <u>Frederick Price</u> or <u>Creflo Dollar</u>! Who can come forth from the prosperity preachers? Could it be <u>Ken Copeland</u> or <u>Hagin</u>? How about <u>Oral or Richard</u>?

Can we find one man in all of Christianity that can prove tithing 10% from the cross of Christ is a <u>New Covenant Command</u> and was a practice of the early church? Will it be <u>Charles Stanley</u>, <u>Jack Hayford,</u> or <u>Jerry Falwell</u>? Can the <u>Pride in Pat Robertson's</u> Wisdom do it? How about false teacher <u>John Avanzini</u>? The <u>Pope</u>?

Surely, with all of the tithes collected in this nation and around the world from bible believing Christians, there is one Christian leader that can document tithing 10% *In My Presence.* Don't hold your breath. You will never see your pastor and myself publicly debate this issue from scripture. He cannot prove that tithing was a New Covenant practice of the early church!

NONE OF THE GURUS LISTED ABOVE WILL EVER PUBLICLY TAKE THE "TITHING CHALLENGE."

Saints, Are You Aware
That The Words
Tithe, Tithes, Or Tithing
Appear
In Only 35 Scriptures?

Were You Also Aware
That God Originally Intended That
Tithing Would <u>Never</u> Involve Money
In The Old Testament?

In The New Testament
There Are Only <u>7</u> Scriptures About Tithes.
<u>Never</u> Is Tithing Used In Relation To You
As A New Testament Saint!

It is rumored that there is a lot of talk about Money in Your Day. In fact many are saying that every time that they enter a church a large amount of time is spent speaking about money. Who has bewitched you that you should fall prey to men that would seek money from you? Have you fallen so far from Grace that you now attempt to justify yourselves again by acts of the flesh?

Brethren, Have You Not Heard?

WHAT TITHING IS REALLY ALL ABOUT?

WHAT WERE THE FATHER'S REAL INTENTIONS

WITH TITHING FROM THE BEGINNING?

HOW DOES IT RELATE TO YOU AS A BELIEVER?

SHOULD THE CHURCH PRACTICE <u>THE LAW OF TITHING</u> TODAY?

Before you respond, I ask you to follow with me through the word of God and look at what tithing was really all about. From the Old Testament to the New Testament, let's search and find out what are the <u>REAL SPIRITUAL PRINCIPLES OF TITHING</u>.

If you will read the scriptures with me; if you will truly search the matter out for yourself, then, the truths you are about to discover will become yours.

Truth in and of Itself
Does not stand by the "opinions of men."
Truth needs no one to declare it as
Truth...

Truth will Bear Witness of Himself.

<u>Worth repeating.</u> "Truth in and of itself does not stand by the "opinions of men." Truth needs no one to declare it as Truth ... for Truth will bear witness of Himself!" As we search many things will become evident along the way. Be aware that you may grow angry at what the "supposed men of God" have done to the integrity of scripture. You will probably become angry with me also for destroying your religious tradition. I assure you that every tithe-collecting pastor or televangelist that practices the law of tithing does so because of their inability to walk by faith and their own desire for personal gain.

How **serious** **is** **this** **study**? How important is it to your faith? This study is foundational in hearing God for yourself. Be honest with yourself. If you cannot hear God in the carnal realm of what to do with your money then you cannot hear God at all. If you practice the law of tithing in any form it will rob you of your faith. How serious is this study? If you will really search this out, no one will ever be able to deceive you in the area of tithing again. Your eyes will be opened to the "Huxters" of our day. Huxters that promote, practice, and preach "The Lie of The Tithe" on YOU.

As we travel from the Old Testament to and through the New Testament I assure you that I will not skirt one issue involving tithes. If you will study with me and read the scriptures, in the end, you will understand the spiritual and foundational principles the Father was laying for his children. We will also look at some other scriptural examples, not directly related to tithing, but used by many charlatans of today as examples of tithing and giving to get. Most of them render a twisted perversion of true scriptural truths.

Along the way I will interject some of my opinion, humor, and direct, open rebuke at those who twist the scriptures for their own benefit. This will be done for two reasons. The first reason being it is time to clean up this filth that we see and hear today proclaiming to be of the Faith of Christ! Secondly, both hypocrisy and heresy are never to be addressed behind closed doors. If they speak publicly then they are to be addressed publicly.

In all of church history both hypocrisy and heresy were never privately addressed. It is time to expose these gurus even if he is your pastor! If our understanding of the law from the Old Testament is off, then our foundational understanding of our Father's heart and his spiritual principles can be missed by us in this critical issue of tithing. We will find that ...

Every act of Tithing Was not about Money!

Have you ever wondered why you can turn on the TV to nearly any Christian program and it will not be too long before the issue of money becomes the main theme? Have you ever asked a non-believer what they see when they flip to a Christian channel? Money ... Money ... Money ... and then at the end of the program, what else, but more money.

You will also find what I call <u>Class Christianity</u> projecting this image before the world over the public airways. 'There are some of you who can give $1000.00 and some of you can give $500.00 and if you don't have $500.00 then just send us $100.00.' The host normally has a varying array of gifts to bestow upon you according to your ability to give. As viewers, many are made to feel inadequate at not being able to give the largest gift. But then we are saved at the last moment by the blanket appeal, 'If you don't have a hundred, just give a $50...even a five or a ten will do...brother! Help us get the gospel out; Remember, you can't out give God.' All of this is done openly before the lost and to the shame of the church!

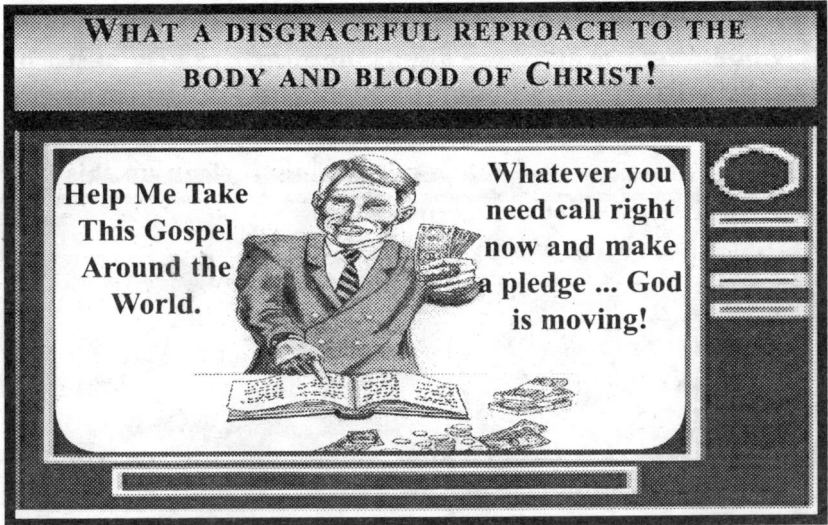

WHAT A DISGRACEFUL REPROACH TO THE BODY AND BLOOD OF CHRIST!

Help Me Take This Gospel Around the World.

Whatever you need call right now and make a pledge ... God is moving!

To understand the disgraceful level these lovers of money have sunken to, imagine watching the Jerry Lewis Telethon as Jerry tells everyone watching to plant a hundred dollar seed in order to receive a hundred fold return.

Think about it...What would it be like if you took all of the gimmicks that you have seen projected by TV preachers and they were used to run the Jerry Lewis Telethon? 'Well, child of God, you just have to trust Ole' Jerry here. This is good ground to sow your seed. If you got a need plant a seed ... Offer a memorial to Ole' Jerry's ministry and God will bless you!

Pat Robertson would offer a founder membership. He is the greatest promoter of Class Christianity before the lost. What is a 700 Club anyhow? Someone needs to investigate the Billions that he stuck in his pocket when he sold the Family Entertainment Channel, which by the way, was paid for by the 700 Club Members. I thought God had told him to develop a Family channel. Do you suppose that God told him to sell out to Fox Television? You need to watch Pat's original videos when he made appeals for money. Then you will see what a spiritual thief he really is! We could go on forever with the foolish quotes they make but I hope you get the point.

The entire nation would rise up in disgust if such practices and methods were used to fund a Jerry Lewis Labor Day Telethon. Yet, we see these disgusting practices being used by most "Christian" (and I use the term lightly) preachers on TV, all to the shame of the church and Christian television.

Jerry Lewis, as well as every other fundraiser for almost any good cause in this nation, operates with greater integrity and honor.

Surely, one day Jan and Paul Crouch will reach the understanding that the gospel was not commissioned by Jesus according to our ability to hold telethons. We are not to beg for money, sit in gold chairs with our hair blown out of proportion, and bleeding mascara in order to get the gospel out. Moses led over a million people without a microphone or a P.A. system, much less a satellite dish and a telethon.

I say it's time to repent, clean up our act, stop acting as if nothing is wrong and realize that Christ Jesus, the Hope of Glory, is being trampled to open shame before the lost! We, by our very actions, are allowing the lost to openly ridicule our King and our Faith because of <u>Our Tolerance</u> of these charlatans and their ungodly fund raising tactics.

> **It is time to speak up, not shut-up.**
> **We must judge within ourselves,**
> **Not those that are without, but those within.**

I challenge each one of you to stand up against the charlatans of our day! Call the TV and radio stations! Stand up in church and ask them to prove their doctrine to be of Christ. Do not sit in apathy another day!

Real love cannot remain silent when it sees injustice, error, false doctrine, impure motives, bondage, guilt, control, and manipulation. All of these things are the tools of the charlatans of our day, including the "Lie of the Tithe," as the chief cornerstone in the falsehood of their deception.

We must make every effort to capture the Real Gospel of Christ within our hearts and project that image before the lost, not the sickened, money-grubbing Class Christianity Jesus that is now being projected before the world.

YOUR PASTOR IS INVOLVED JUST AS MUCH,

IF NOT MORE,

THAN THE TELEVANGELIST.

Tithes are not Tithes.

Remember, we are going to search for money. It is critical at this point that you determine within your heart to read every scripture that we look at in our study. Let the Truth found in scripture build your foundation and not the crafty opinions of man.

Our 21st century millennium mentality has been programmed by the religious pulpit to believe that Tithing involved money. In our study we will find that tithing **NEVER** involved money. Most people think that tithes, money, and offerings in the bible were all one and the same thing. Actually, they are not; each had its own distinct purpose as we will discover. <u>Double Read The Underlined.</u>

Deut 12:11-27

11   "then there will be the place where the LORD your God chooses to make His name abide. There you shall bring all that I command you: your burnt offerings, your sacrifices, your tithes, the heave offerings of your hand, and all your choice offerings which you vow to the LORD.

12   "And you shall rejoice before the LORD your God, you and your sons and your daughters, your male and female servants, and the Levite who is within your gates, <u>since he has no portion nor inheritance with you.</u>

13   "Take heed to yourself that you do not offer your burnt offerings in every place that you see;

14   "but in the place which the LORD chooses, in one of your tribes, there you shall offer your burnt offerings, and there you shall do all that I command you.

15   "<u>However, you may slaughter and eat meat within all your gates, whatever your heart desires, according to the blessing of the LORD your God which He has given you;</u> the unclean and the clean may eat of it, of the gazelle and the deer alike.

16   "Only you shall not eat the blood; you shall pour it on the earth like water.

17 "You may not eat within your gates the tithe of your grain or your new wine or your oil, of the firstlings of your herd or your flock, of any of your offerings which you vow, of your freewill offerings, or of the heave offering of your hand.

18 **"But you must eat them before the LORD your God** in the place which the LORD your God chooses, you and your son and your daughter, your male servant and your female servant, and the Levite who is within your gates; and you shall rejoice before the LORD your God in all to which you put your hands.

19 "Take heed to yourself that you do not forsake the Levite as long as you live in your land.

20 "When the LORD your God enlarges your border as He has promised you, and you say, 'Let me eat meat,' because you long to eat meat, you may eat as much meat as your heart desires.

21 **"If the place where the LORD your God chooses to put His name is too far from you, then you may slaughter from your herd and from your flock which the LORD has given you, just as I have commanded you, and you may eat within your gates as much as your heart desires.**

22 "Just as the gazelle and the deer are eaten, so you may eat them; the unclean and the clean alike may eat them.

23 "Only be sure that you do not eat the blood, for the blood is the life; you may not eat the life with the meat.

24 "You shall not eat it; you shall pour it on the earth like water.

25 "You shall not eat it, that it may go well with you and your children after you, when you do what is right in the sight of the LORD.

26 "Only the holy things which you have, and your vowed offerings, you shall take and go to the place which the LORD chooses.

27 "And you shall offer your burnt offerings, the meat and the blood, on the altar of the LORD your God; and the blood of your sacrifices shall be poured out on the altar of the LORD your God, **and you shall eat the meat.**

(NKJ)

Foundational   Understanding

Of The Law As It Was Given To Moses

Tithes are not Tithes. <u>Remember, we are going to search for money.</u> It is important that we understand the basic functions of how money, tithes, sacrifices, and free will offerings flowed through the temple.

THERE WERE FOUR BASIC FUNCTIONS WITHIN THE TEMPLE THAT WERE RELATED TO TITHES, SACRIFICES, OFFERINGS, AND MONEY IN THE TEMPLE.

Deuteronomy, Chapter 12:6
"There *you* shall take your burnt offerings, your sacrifices, your tithes, the heave offerings of your hand, <u>your vowed offerings, your freewill offerings</u>, and the firstborn of your herds and flocks.
(NKJ)

First There was an offering or a vow; a <u>free will offering</u> which meant you could offer it freely or not at all (also see vs.6). A free will offering was just that, an act of your own free will.   Think on this ... How could you rob God of something that He left up to you to do <u>as an act of your own free will</u>?

Second The sacrifice or the "Holy Tithe" was for sin. (Deut 12:26) Even this was to be EATEN BY THE TITHER!

"Only the holy things which you have, and your vowed offerings, you shall take and go to the place which the LORD chooses. (NKJ) Even That Was Eaten by the Tither!

Third The Temple Tax. (Exodus 30:11-16). I recommend you read these passages also. The money paid in the temple tax was the same for the rich and the poor, but you had to be 20 years old before you were required to pay it. It was not a tithe, but a tax that was used to operate the temple. (pay the light bill). This Tax was for the Temple ... Not The Church!

Exodus 30:11-15

11   Then the LORD spoke to Moses, saying:

12   "When you take the census of the children of Israel for their number, then every man shall give a ransom for himself to the LORD, when you number them, that there may be no plague among them when you number them.

13   "This is what everyone among those who are numbered shall give: half a shekel according to the shekel of the sanctuary (a shekel is twenty gerahs). The half-shekel shall be an offering to the LORD.

14   "Everyone included among those who are numbered, from twenty years old and above, shall give an offering to the LORD.

15   "The rich shall not give more and the poor shall not give less than half a shekel,

Fourth The "Actual Tithe" was taken to the temple by the tither and Was Eaten in the presence of the Father. We shall see that this "Tithe" was Not always eaten in the temple. The Father also trusted the tither. The tither did not always have to come to the temple; he was allowed to stay home and EAT THE TITHE WITHIN HIS OWN GATES!

Has Anyone
Ever Told You
That You
WereTo Eat
Your Tithe?

From Chapter 12, if we read nothing into it and add nothing to it, we can see that what the Father wanted was communion with His children. He desired His children to recognize that He was the Sovereign Source of all Substance in their lives. Their inability to learn how to rest in this sovereign understanding was the reason the children of Israel wandered through the desert for 40 years. We can see that tithing was about thanksgiving, relationship, fellowship, and communion with the Father. It was not about money, or giving to get, or planting seeds in hope of a hundred fold return. The simple act of communion and fellowship with the Father was at the center of His heart. You will begin to understand what Real Faith is about before we are finished. Who is the man that can give God one thing or add to his account?

The Father desired His children to come and sup with Him, and in so doing, He would receive glory unto Himself. My, how good it is when the children grow to maturity and recognize the Father's hand of provision and stop to say, "Thanks Dad, I recognize all you have done to help me." The sweetest table is communion with the Father. What earthly father would "require" an offering or tithe of his children? Even as earthly fathers is it not genuine communion and fellowship with our children that we desire the most?

Before we look at our next passage, look one more time at two important verses in

Deut 12:Verse 12 & 19.

12   "And you shall rejoice before the LORD your God, you and your sons and your daughters, your male and female servants, and the Levite who is within your gates, <u>since he has no portion nor inheritance with you.</u>

19   "Take heed to yourself that you <u>do not forsake the Levite</u> as long as you live in your land. (NKJ)

Notice that the Father clearly says that the Levite (vs. 12) has no portion or inheritance with you. Then in vs. 19 He says take heed you do not forsake the Levite. (<u>Remember this for later on.</u>)

When you begin to see the real meaning of tithing I hope you will understand how much it grieves the Father's heart to see and hear the charlatans of our day prostituting the gospel for a buck. The children of God are to be salt and light. The Children of the Kingdom of Christ are not to be beggars, always asking for money to stay on the air waves, or for help to pay the church mortgage. <u>We are not called to public bake sales, church garage sales, car washes, or fundraisers.</u> <u>We are called to a higher demonstration.</u>

"Show Me the Money"

You shall Know Them By Their Fruits

By faith and integrity we are to demonstrate to the world that we have the one true God. Wake up people!

I believe all of what we see is rooted within the issues of Pride, Greed, and Servanthood to Mammon. Seed Faith, Church Tithes, Blessings, and Cursings etc. all flourish because of a lack of understanding of the Father's heart and Pulpit Greed.

Let me say that there are many men in this nation that stand in a pulpit and know the truth of what you are about to see. However, they refuse to be honest and truthful with you. Because of their own greedy hearts and personal agendas they willingly choose to leave people in the bondage of the law.

In the late 1980s I spent several months attending meetings at a self-professed prophet's home by the name of Kent Simpson. I grew to respect some of Kent's theology and the parts that I did not understand I asked God for revelation.

I remember calling Kent a few years later with a question about tithing. I was having some Friday night meetings in my home and a woman desperately needed an eye operation. Without it she would go blind.

There were about 30 to 40 people present so I asked everyone to contribute. To my surprise, after everyone left all I found in the basket was about three dollars. I was stunned and heart broken at the cold hardness of the people. I did not understand how people who say they know God could not give anything for a woman's eyes. Everyone seemed to like the word and food that I freely supplied, but where was their compassion? The next day I called Kent Simpson.

"Why would people do this?" I asked him. Kent asked me if I preached tithing. I told him I could not preach it because tithing was not biblical and I did not believe in it. His answer revealed his heart and immediately removed him from having any influence in my life. Kent replied, "It does not matter if it's biblical or even if you do not believe in it … It Works!" I hung up the phone stunned and amazed at his words. This self proclaimed prophet had just violated the Truth and Integrity of scripture for money. As I look back I think that Kent actually practiced more sorcery than prophecy. Every pastor knows the truth about tithing. If they deny it they are not Of the Spirit of Truth! They are no different than Kent.

I promise you that if you keep a teachable heart and search the matter out for yourself you will see the truth. Don't take my word for it! Read the scriptures and anything else you think connects to this subject. I know if you do this that your faith will explode and a Tangible Reality of Christ will become evident in your faith. You will not be easily deceived again.

I recommend that you read Deuteronomy Chapter 12 in its entirety. Remember that this is the Law as God gave it to Moses. One of the first simple things we can observe ... and I ask you to take note; do not forget this point:

There Is No Money Involved!
Do not forget that statement!

THE TITHE,
As it was Directly Related to The Old Testament Practitioner Under the Law, ...

Never
Involved Money!
The "Tithe was Always Eaten" By the Tither.
Or, The Tithe was given To others In the form of food.

IT WAS NOT

Because they had no money, because in fact, they did, as we will see in a moment.

Why would the Father require His people to eat a meal In His Presence?

Why didn't God tell them
To come and give 10% of their income
As most are told to do today?

Dropping money in a basket or a plate is a cold hearted act of man's own devices. It is not the close fellowship of faith that Your Father desired you to have with Him.

Dropping Money In A Plate Does Not

Prove That You Know God!

It <u>Proves</u> <u>Your</u> <u>Inability</u> <u>To</u> <u>Hear</u> <u>God!</u>

We are going to look at numerous scriptures that will prove tithing was not about money. We will also look at many examples in scripture that will prove tithing and the spiritual principles involved were about one thing alone ... communion with the Father.

Once again, has anyone ever told you that you were to EAT YOUR TITHE? What preacher has ever stood behind a pulpit and told you that the tithe was to be eaten by you, the tither? Don't tell me times have changed ... God is still the same! <u>How may I ask are you, as a tither, giving God anything if the Father wanted you to Eat the Tithe?</u>

Think with me. If you were to eat the tithe, how could you ever be charged with robbing God? What was the tithe all about and what was the Father's heart in this critical foundational principle? What issues of <u>Faith</u> are involved?

Now You Tithe

Now You Don't

Deuteronomy 14:22

"You shall truly tithe all
the <u>INCREASE</u> of your
grain that the field produces
year by year.

Here we find another foundational
Spiritual Principle
From the Father's Heart
Regarding Tithing in verse 22.
The Father <u>NEVER</u> required anyone to tithe while
they were on the decreasing scale in life. Tithing
was only to be practiced by the tither while life was
on the increasing scale.

<u>Not one time in</u>

<u>ALL of scripture</u>

<u>Will you ever find</u>

<u>God asking people</u>

<u>To tithe on the</u>

<u>Decreasing Scale!</u>

How many sermons have you heard from the pulpit or television about giving your last two cents or giving out of your need? The example most charismatics normally use is the example with the widow woman in Matthew who threw in her last two mites. I assure you that is not what happened there. When we get to the New Testament we will see what really happened with the widow's mites. We will also prove that the early church practiced this spiritual principle of tithing <u>only on the increase</u>. Remember that tithing was not about money.

Nowhere in scripture are we ever told to tithe while your life is on the decreasing scale. The mentality echoed from a Baptist pulpit is, "You need to trust God, pay God first. Why I have been tithing all of my life. In the good times and especially during the hard times and tithing works." Every Baptist pulpit has echoed that statement. Their mentality is that when times are tough financially it must be some kind of test of your faith. Just hang in there and keep tithing and God will eventually fix your problem. <u>To even consider that God would test a monetary tither is ludicrous!</u>

I CHALLENGE YOU
TO FIND ONE TIME IN SCRIPTURE
WHERE THE TITHE
WAS EVER PRACTICED ON THE DECREASE!

"Give out of your need, child of God," as John Avanzini would say. Where do they get this dark theology? It resides in the chambers of their filthy, greedy, and UN-Christ like hearts. It is evident their Hearts are filled with every kind of trickery and impure motive. They will say and do anything in an effort to make sure that they take home the moneybag, just like Judas! Nearly every telethon on TBN is full of John Avanzini's deceptive fund-raising tactics. Jan and Paul love his ability to raise money with the promise of a harvest. You must give out of your want in order to get something back. I venture to say that most of you are still waiting for the "harvest" to come in!

IF YOU ARE BAPTIST
YOU THINK TITHING "WORKS"
YOU ARE RIGHT
IT IS MAN'S RELIGIOUS WORKS!

Deuteronomy 14:22-26

22   "You shall truly tithe all the <u>INCREASE</u> of your grain that the field produces year by year.

23   "<u>And you shall eat before the LORD your God</u>, in the place where He chooses to make His name abide, the tithe of your grain and your new wine and your oil, of the firstborn of your herds and your flocks, that you may learn to fear the LORD your God always.

24   "<u>But if the journey is too long for you, so that you are not able to carry the tithe,</u> or if the place where the LORD your God chooses to put His name is too far from you, when the LORD your God has blessed you,

25   "<u>then you shall exchange it for money</u>, take the money in your hand, and go to the place which the LORD your God chooses.

26   "<u>And you shall spend that money for whatever your heart desires:</u> for oxen or sheep, for wine or similar drink, <u>for whatever your heart desires; you shall eat there before the LORD your God</u>, and you shall rejoice, you and your household. (NKJ)

What Earthly Father Would
Require Payment From His
Own Children
During Hard
Times?

Why Would You
Perceive God
Your Father
To Be This way?

Saints, Your Father Has Always Trusted You With The Tithe!

Read with Me
In Deut. verses 24-26

24   "But if the journey is too long for you, so that you are not able to carry the tithe, or if the place where the LORD your God chooses to put His name is too far from you, when the LORD your God has blessed you,

25"<u>then you shall exchange it for money,</u> take the money in your hand, and go to the place which the LORD your God chooses.

26   "And you shall **SPEND THAT MONEY** for whatever your heart desires: for oxen or sheep, for wine or similar drink, <u>for whatever your heart desires</u>; <u>you shall eat there before the</u>

<u>LORD</u> <u>your God</u>, and you shall rejoice, you and your household. (NKJ)

The Father shows us again that the tithe was not about money. <u>He allowed the Tither to $ell the Tithe</u>. This is in total contradiction to everything we here today! We have become so programmed that tithing is about money from the pulpit when all of scripture proves, It Is Not!

"<u>Turn The Tithe into Money</u>," then come, and buy the best of everything. Whatever your heart desires buy it and come fellowship with me. Come and have a meal with me, rejoice before me, you and your household. God also declares that they can have a strong drink if they desire. After traveling all of that way they probably needed one.

Have you traded Intimate Fellowship with God

For some
Cold Religious Systems

Man Made Offering Plate?

Sell the Tithe
Come And Buy The Best of Everything
Whatever Your Heart Desires
Come and Have A Meal With Me
Rejoice Before Me

Why didn't God say just bring your money and put it in the basket? Why not just send the Money to the Temple via UPS or FedEx? Remember, don't forget to pay your tithes while you are away on "VACATION" is a common pulpit statement. Is this the God you have? Money in a Plate proves you do not know Him. You are being Robbed by man made religious tradition! What is even more important in this passage is the simple fact that God <u>TRUSTED</u> the tither with the responsibility of handling the tithe. It was not under the supervision of a Priest.

The Father has always trusted His children with the tithe. <u>It was the Levites in the Old Testament, as well as, the New Levites of Our Day that He does not trust.</u>

This is why God defined the Levites portion as being *SEPARATE* from the tither.

SPEND THE MONEY AND EAT
WHATEVER YOUR HEART DESIRES!
I Don't know About You .... But As For Me

RIGHT NOW ... I AM HUNGRY
FOR A PLATE OF LEVITE!

DEUTERONOMY 14: 27-29

27   "You shall not forsake the Levite who is within your gates, **for he has no part nor inheritance with** 𝕪𝕠𝕦.
28   "At the end of every third year you shall bring out the tithe of your produce of that year and store it up within your gates.
29   And the Levite, **because he has no portion nor inheritance with** 𝕪𝕠𝕦, and the stranger and the fatherless and the widow who are within your gates, may come and eat and be satisfied, that the Lord your God may bless you in all the work of your hand which you do.

In verse 27 the Father says, "Do not forsake the Levite." In the same verse he also declares that the Levite has no portion or inheritance with you. In verse 28 the tither is told to distribute what he has stored up to those within his gates. Verse 29 clearly defines, where and with whom, the Levite's portion and identity was to be. **LOOK** at those with whom the Levite was to be identified: the stranger, the fatherless, and the widow.

The Father ordained that the priesthood would be identified with the needy of the earth. Just as Jesus came to seek and save those who were lost, the Father required that the Levitical priesthood would be identified with the less fortunate.

Every third year when the Tither
Was to bring the tithe out of their storehouses,
Look what else happened.

The Tithe NEVER WENT to the Temple!

It was distributed to the Levite, the stranger, the fatherless, and the widow. The Levite priest would give the food to these people as the God of the tither was glorified. <u>The stranger, the fatherless, the widow, and the poor of the earth would stand back and proclaim that surely you must have the One True God.</u>

> GOD WAS RECEIVING GLORY
> UNTO HIMSELF
> AS HIS PROVISION
> WAS BEING DEMONSTRATED
> THROUGH THE LIVES OF HIS
> CHILDREN.

The tithe was **NOT TO BE STORED** up for possible hard times in the future. In fact, quite the opposite was taking place. The storehouses were emptied in order to keep the tither living a life of faith; in total recognition that God alone was to be their Sovereign Source of Provision.

We will also see this principle in the New Testament. Imagine emptying your accounts every three years and giving your surplus to the needy within your city. Imagine starting over at ground zero every three years. This practice required the tither to live a life of faith totally dependent on God. It also kept the practitioner's heart from being captured by the things of this world. When anyone builds bigger barns in order to store up and hoard $ubstance, you move from faith to fear.

Just as important is the fact that all of this took place *within* the town or gates of the tither.

Deuteronomy 26: 11-13

11   "So you shall rejoice in every good thing which the LORD your God has given to you and your house, you and the Levite and the stranger who is among you.

12   "When you have finished laying aside all the tithe of your increase in the third year-- the year of tithing-- **and have given it to the Levite, the stranger, the fatherless, and the widow, so that they may eat within your gates and be filled,**

13   "then you shall say before the LORD your God: 'I have removed the holy tithe from my house, and also **have given them to the Levite, the stranger, the fatherless, and the widow, according to all Your commandments which You have commanded me**; I have not transgressed Your commandments, nor have I forgotten them.(NKJ)

We still have not found anything to do with money...

And We Will Not!

The Levites Portion and Identity
Was to be with the Widow, Orphan, & Stranger.

The Father <u>ordained</u> that the priesthood would be identified with the needy of the earth. Just as Jesus came to seek and save those who were lost, the Father required that the Levitical priesthood would be identified with the less fortunate.

This Was His Identity.
He Has No Portion Or Inheritance
With You.

What about your Levite; who does he identify with?

Tithing was not about money. It was about communion with the Father and the Father receiving glory unto Himself. <u>God Received Glory</u> from the obedient acts of faith and kindness that were expressed through the lives of His children.

We can also see that the Father has an answer to the homeless problem. God has a welfare system better than any governmental program. The church needs to walk in the foundational principles we see here, and demonstrate a living reality of their faith in God.

The stranger, the fatherless, and the widow were to be taken care of by the children of God. The institutionalized church of our day has forfeited the Glory due to the Father.

They have exchanged that Glory for building programs, ballparks, family life centers, and massive sanctuaries for concerts and one-hour sermons. Most people think a family life center is a place for juice and cookies after church. This is all a direct result of a false tithing mentality produced by crafty businessmen standing behind a pulpit. In reality, the Father desires to express Himself to the community *through* the lives of His children. Wake up people!

These scriptures help illustrate how the Father was receiving Glory unto Himself and how the Levite was to be at the level of those who had need. He was clearly to be identified with them. This is why his portion was appointed with them. Oddly enough, the New Levites of our day are the same as those in Jesus' day. They were the wealthiest class of the children of God, as are, the majority of church leaders today. The practice of the "Lie of The Tithe" by the church today is largely responsible for this illusion that we call a church. Many think that because they see large buildings and numbers that this is a move of God. "Surely God must be moving here!"

Let me warn you. The Holy Spirit works all by Himself. He alone has the power and the ability to enter a bar and convict a drunk on a barstool about the error of his ways. Just because the Spirit goes into the bar and convicts a sinner on a barstool that does not justify the bar! In the same manner, the Holy Spirit can enter a building filled with people shouting praises to God and convict a sinner sitting in a pew about the error of his ways. That does not justify the Institutionalized church you attend. Is there any difference between the Holy Spirit entering the bar and entering your church?

You will find the Spirit showing up More often in the Bar!

The Holy Spirit will be found working in the highways and byways seeking the lost, not the self-righteous! Just like Jesus he will only enter the temple to redeem someone or <u>rebuke the leadership!</u> Most churches have become nothing more than an emotional counseling center anyway. A mere club in Christian City!

How many Building Programs have been $old To congregations as a Step of Faith?

Faith has nothing to do with what we see. Most preachers have taken members into debt with commitment pledges for a building fund.

All of this is done under the false religious banner of "Reaching their community for the Lord!" Yet, for the most part, our communities remain the same. It does not take a brain surgeon to recognize that the moral condition of society in this nation is on a major downhill spiral.

I am convinced By the Lord that the majority of what we see is nothing more than the flesh of man. Nearly everything we see has been built by the crafty businessmen of our day with bloated egos desiring to show the community in which they live that they are the "real man" of God in the city.

They are Masters at using the Law of Tithing coupled with the tools of guilt and condemnation on the children of God. As a result, we now have corporate church U.S.A. where the members come and go without any Reality of Christ Truly being imparted to their inward being. It is a system totally void of the Reality of what True Faith in Christ is really about.

This Corporate Church of our generation is still holding members captive on the pew, members who come and go for years whose lives are void of purpose and real destiny. Christians who are unable to demonstrate to the world a tangible Reality of the God they serve.

The next time you become angry at the Media or someone who makes fun of Christianity, just turn to the nearest Christian channel and observe the disgrace. Better yet, ask a non believer what they see and hear on TV and the Church.

HOW CAN ANY MAN IMPART TRUE FAITH TO YOU WHEN HIS "WORKS" ARE BUILT BY THE LAW, <u>APART</u> FROM REAL GRACE AND FAITH!

THE HARDEST THING YOU WILL EVER DO IS TO BE HONEST WITH YOURSELF!

If you cannot hear the Spirit every week in what or to whom you are to give, face it, you cannot hear Him.

> If you cannot hear Him in the *CARNAL REALM*
> Of what you are to do with your filthy money
> Why do you think you can hear Him
> In the Deeper Spiritual Matters?
>
> I urge you to prove to yourself
> That you can hear Him.
> Do not give another Thin Dime until you know
> Where and to Whom He wants you to give.

Then, if you will walk in that maturity, the flesh of man will fall away and what will be built ... Will Be Built by the Spirit with Christ as head. God will never tell you to underwrite a reprobate system that walks apart from true biblical faith. If the pulpit endorses tithes in any manner, it is in total reprobation. The Word Is True to Himself. A lot more than money is at issue here. The Bible declares, "Faith comes by Hearing."

When you practice the law of tithing your actions are an open expression of your inability to hear God. If you depart from the law and learn how to really hear God, the dead god you now have will become alive. You must become totally honest with yourself, admitting that you can or cannot hear God.

It is sad how the corporate church and the shallow leaders (I call them the "culprits in the pulpits") have become masters at getting your money. Yet, they have failed to disciple one generation on how to Really Hear God for themselves.

These Culprits live in fear that their little illusion will collapse. They will not walk humble enough to live at the level of the Widow, Orphan, or the Stranger. Which one has told you that the tither ate the tithe? When has your pastor stood and told you that tithing was **_NEVER_** about money? He will not teach you that you have a <u>Serious Spiritual Responsibility</u> to learn to hear God for yourself.

He will not tell you that the foundation of all Faith comes ONLY in your ability to hear God and that begins when you know Him as Sovereign Source! You must allow your Father to touch the lives of those around You!

"Emasculated" Cheerleader!

"Do not give <u>Another</u> <u>Dime</u> until you learn to hear God."
Are you justified by your tithing?
No flesh will be justified in His sight!

Have you ever felt guilty when you heard the preacher say, "Will a man rob God?" If you are a religious tither, I assure you that you live with an ongoing mental account of every dollar that comes into your life. You will always make sure that God gets His 10%. You walk and live with that mental attitude. God forbid that you should die and you owed God money! Bondage and law are your masters, not faith! Congratulations! The masters of manipulation and control from the pulpit have accomplished and built this entire mental attitude within you.

Many like to tithe 10% because, frankly, it is a whole lot easier than facing the real facts about their faith. The real issue, as I said, is not tithing but hearing God in what and to whom you are to give. Why, what would you do if He told you to give it all and follow Him? I see; it is a whole lot easier for you just to give 10%! The religious rich like the tithe because they can live with it.

The Religious Rich like the tithe because they can live with it.

This is why they embrace the prosperity gospel; it justifies their legal rights for hoarding and their storehouses.

This is why they embrace the prosperity gospel; it justifies their legal rights for hoarding and their storehouses. No one really believes what Jesus said about having treasure in heaven anymore. He instructed the rich young ruler to sell it all and give it to the poor. He did not say just part of what he had or what was convenient, but all!

Jesus said, "You cannot serve God and mammon." He did not say part time or a little bit … He said, "You cannot!" Not one disciple served for money. Not one apostle was in it for a pension or a Mercedes and a large home. Find it in the book!

Do you realize that the charlatans of our day, along with their false doctrine, actually have led many to believe that the power of getting the gospel out has been given over to the power of mammon? Let me remind you and them. The power of getting the gospel out has one agent: the Holy Spirit alone. He does not need the filthy lucre of Mammon or man's flesh to get it done. Jesus said, "No man comes unto the Father, except the Spirit draw him."

If you attend a church where money Is no longer an issue, **Congratulations,** The **Counterfeit** has been accepted as the <u>Original!</u>

So far, we have found that none of our Father's original intentions had anything to do with money at all. It was about communion with the Father and your recognition of Him as the Sovereign Source of all substance in your life. Tithing was also about giving to the strangers, the widows, and the orphans in your land so that the Father received <u>Glory</u> unto Himself. Even the Levitical priest that was supported by the tither was to be identified with the stranger, the widow, and the orphan. It was to demonstrate to those within your community that surely <u>YOU</u> have the one true God.

Saints, Remember This

It is <u>Impossible</u> to Rob God of natural substance!
It is <u>Possible</u> to Rob God of the Glory due Him from being expressed through your life.

CONSIDER WHAT IS SAID AND FEAR THE LATTER STATEMENT.

My, how the church has missed it! The desires of the Father's heart were made known to them through the laws of the Old Covenant. Today, the desire of His heart is still the same. New Covenant living is not to embrace one single letter of the law. The church should still take care of the widows, orphans, and strangers within its own community. The church has forfeited this privilege to the government and its welfare systems. WAIT until we get to the New Testament. It will get even clearer.

NOT ONE TIME ...
DID WE EVER COLLECT TITHES
NOT ONE TIME ...
DID WE EVER PASS A PLATE
NOT ONE TIME ...
DID I EVER PREACH ON MONEY

For the years that I was pastor of a Church and school, not one time did we ever collect tithes! Not one time did we ever pass a basket. Not one time did I ever preach about Money.

Those who came were released to hear God for themselves. I was determined that if we stood it would be by the Power of God and not by the crafty practices of man's wicked heart. As a result those who came grew in their faith. With a Clear Conscience I can honestly say that everyone who came through those doors were changed forever.

Not one serious seeker who came or was just passing through will ever fit into the reprobate corporate religious system again. Sadly, there were some who missed their purpose and destiny. In every case it was due to Headship and or Worldly desires.

The most asked question the religious crowd would ask me was ... How do you survive? How do you keep your doors open? To which I always responded ... Have you ever heard of a thing called Faith? <u>Shall we be afraid to lose buildings and crowds in exchange for the opportunity of possessing and demonstrating a Reality of Christ!</u>

This desperate generation is in need of a Clear Voice and the sound of a Pure Trumpet sounding a Pure Call! Not a call of Proclamation only ... But a call by Demonstration!

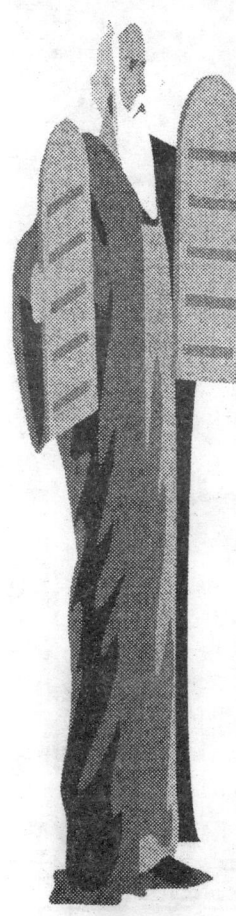

We are The Generation
That must stand and clean up this mess!

Our lives must become "Living Epistles" And Open demonstrations To a Desperate Generation In search of the Truth.

I ASSURE YOU that every church leader who reads this book will have a heart gripped in fear. I say let their deceptive practices fall to the ground. Cursed be the man that perverts the Truth! To them I say REPENT and walk in the Truth. Let the flesh and pride of what man has built come to ashes in order that we might gain a Reality of Christ!

Thanks for Listening

The next time you hear a Religious Tither say, "Don't tell me Tithing Doesn't work, why I've been Tithing 30 years!"...

Tell Him

Circumcision "<u>Works</u>" Also Practice All of the Law!

Present-Day Tithing
Is nothing more Than
"Circumcision"
Of the Wallet!

<u>By</u> <u>the</u> <u>way</u>, Pray for the little boy on the Pew for his Dad to make the right decision.

Now let's turn to Genesis 14 in our study. When you study always look for the first mention of your topic in scripture. Scholars call this "the Origin of the first mention." This will normally have some foundational principles or will add understanding to your study. With that said, let us see what we can learn from the very first tither in all of scripture, Father Abraham.

The Purity Of Abraham's Faith

Pure Heart, Pure Motives
This Is Why He Is Called
The Father of Faith!

Abraham never paid Tithes as you have been told. His heart was not gripped by money or religion. I fear that many behind the pulpit as well as the pew have had their hearts seized with covetousness. Look with me at the real issues of this tithe that was paid to this Priest Melchizedek. Come and see the Deep Spiritual Significance in this meeting between Abraham and Melchizedek. Remember, eyes that are trained on the natural substances will only see the natural. May your heart and Spiritual eyes be opened.

In Chapter 14 we find a story of a war that had broken out in the region between several kings. Abraham received word that his nephew, Lot, had been taken captive. So Father Abraham armed his servants and along with some allies Aner, Eshcol, and Mamre went to free Lot.

Abraham goes to war and later we find that God clearly gives him the victory. He defeats every evil king involved in the wars and captures, not only all of the people, but all of the "spoils of war." As Abraham returns none other than the king of Sodom and Gomorrah meet him at the King's Valley. At the same time that Abraham is returning from the war there appears yet another individual, a priest named Melchizedek, king of Salem (interpreted king of peace). In verse 18 this priest Melchizedek is clearly called the priest of God most high. In verse 20 Abraham gave him a tithe of all "the spoils of war."

Gen 14:16-24
READ ... READ ...READ ... READ

16 So he brought back all the goods, and also brought back his brother Lot and his goods, as well as the women and the people.

17 And the king of Sodom went out to meet him at the Valley of Shaveh (that is, the King's Valley), after his return from the defeat of Chedorlaomer and the kings who were with him.

18 Then Melchizedek king of Salem brought out bread and wine; he was the priest of God Most High.

19 And he blessed him and said:

"Blessed be Abram of God Most High, Possessor of heaven and earth;

20 And blessed be God Most High, Who has delivered your enemies into your hand." And he gave him a tithe of all.

21 Now the king of Sodom said to Abram, "Give me the persons, and take the goods for yourself."

22 But Abram said to the king of Sodom, "I have raised my hand to the LORD, God Most High, the Possessor of heaven and earth,

23 that I will take nothing, from a thread to a sandal strap, and that I will not take anything that is yours, lest you should say, 'I have made Abram rich'--

24 except only what the young men have eaten, and the portion of the men who went with me: Aner, Eshcol, and Mamre; let them take their portion." NKJV

Let me ask you a question
Before we go any further.
What did Abraham give Melchizedek
Out of his own pocket?

Not <u>one</u> Thin Dime!

Take a look again at verses 22-23.

22 _But Abram said to the king of Sodom, "I have raised my hand to the LORD, God Most High, the Possessor of heaven and earth,_
23 that **I will take nothing,** from a thread to a sandal strap, and that I will not take anything that is yours, lest you should say, 'I have made Abram rich'--

We can see that Abraham had already lifted his hand to God and promised that he would take nothing from the "spoils of war." Lest the king of Sodom could say he had made Abraham rich. We see that Abraham was content with knowing God as his source. Abraham realized that everything that came into his life was a sovereign act of God. The victory was God's and we must conclude that Abraham was not in it for the Money, much less the bondage of paying Tithes. Abraham was not going to reach into his pocket for one thin dime in order to justify his Flesh.

THE MORE IMPORTANT QUESTION
WHY WOULD THIS PRIEST MELCHIZEDEK ACCEPT SUCH A TITHE?

If we look at God's commands back in Deuteronomy and Numbers, we can see that the Levitical priesthood was commanded not to accept anything but a perfect spotless sacrifice as an offering.

The lamb, pointing to a type and shadow of Christ, had to be the first born. It had to be perfect on the exterior without spot or blemish. After inspecting the animal for exterior blemishes, they would kill it and begin a complete inspection on the internal organs. Even the internal intestines were checked by hand for tumors or defects. *If any defect was found anywhere on the inside the entire sacrifice would be discarded.*

All of this was pointing
To Christ and His Sinless Perfection.

Unlike The Levitical Priesthood

This Melchizedek, Priest of the Most High God, would accept tithes from the filth of the "spoils of a war," unlike the Levitical priesthood that would follow. No other priesthood would ever touch such filth as the goods of Sodom and Gomorrah. What kind of a Priest of the Most High God Was This Melchizedek?

This priest Melchizedek was declared to be a priest of the Most High God, a priest before there was a Levitical priesthood after the Law. This Priest Melchizedek is the FIRST Priest to appear in ALL of Scripture. His Official Title was "Priest of God Most High." That alone should stir the heart of a seeker to inquire of God for understanding and wisdom concerning this Melchizedek.

This Priest Melchizedek met with Abraham and not only accepted tithes, BUT UNCLEAN TITHES. This Melchizedek accepted the filth of the "spoils of war," the filthy goods of Sodom and Gomorrah as a Tithe. It was a Tithe that Abraham clearly said, "I have nothing to do with this!" Abraham realized that a lot more than Tithes was taking place. The Glory of God was involved in his victory and "I will NOT Touch the Glory!" "I have raised my hand to the LORD, God Most High, the Possessor of heaven and earth,that I will take nothing."

This priest Melchizedek appears out of nowhere and sets up a table with bread and wine and says, "Abraham, come let's have a meal together." This is his one and only appearance in all of scripture. The bible declares that this Priest Melchizedek was without earthly lineage. Without Father, without Mother, without genealogy, having neither beginning of days nor the end of life, but made like the Son of God, remains a priest continually. (Hebrews 7:3)

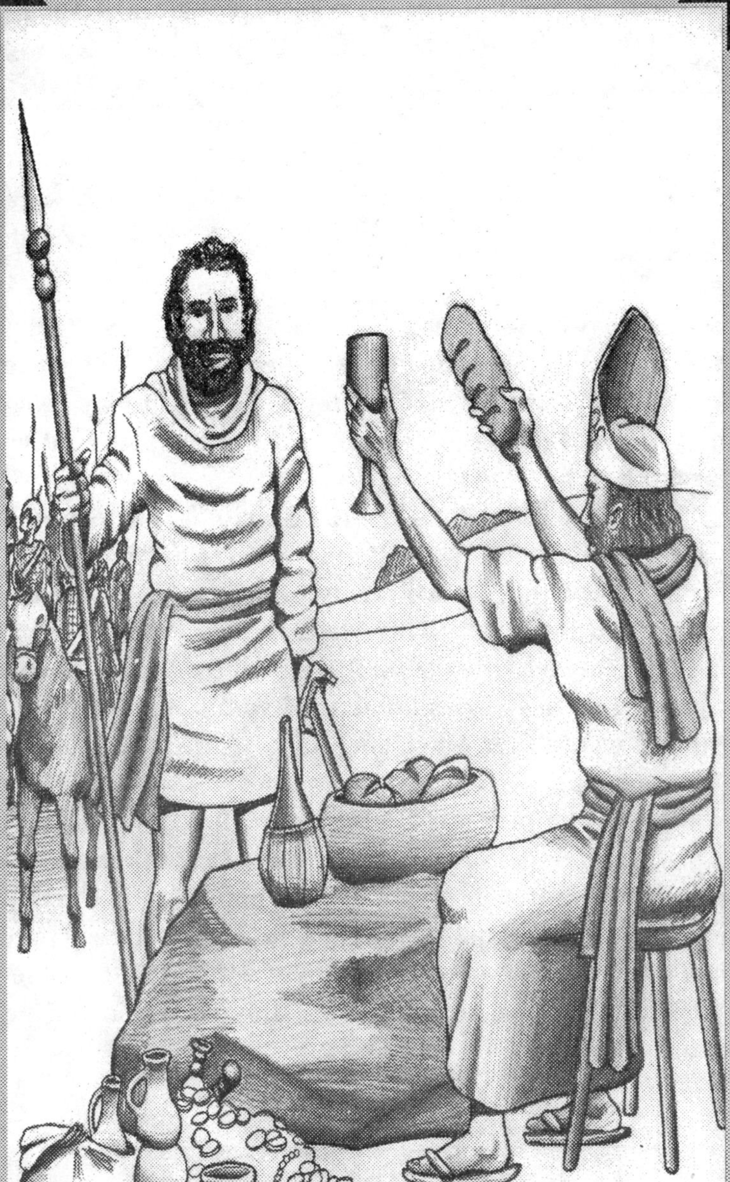

"Thou art a Priest Forever After the Order Of Melchizedek."

As David, the psalmist, said in Psalms 110:5, "Thou art a priest forever after the order of Melchizedek." The writer of Hebrews would also say in Chapter 5, "I have many things to say about this Melchizedek which are hard to be uttered seeing you are dull of hearing."

This Melchizedek is a clear Spiritual picture of Jesus Himself. There would be only one other priesthood in all of scripture that would set up a communion table of bread and wine. It would be Jesus! This Melchizedek, Priest of the Most High God, accepted tithes from the filth of the "spoils of a war," unlike the Levitical priesthood that would follow. No other priesthood would ever touch such filth, as the goods of Sodom and Gomorrah.

Most who meet this High Priest called Jesus today meet Him in the same manner as those who were taken captive in this war. Normally, it is at that critical point in life, where most have had their personal lives taken captive and destroyed by the evil kings of sin. The sin and filth of a life spoiled by the war of life is all we have to offer Him; this is the only tithe He accepts.

This Priesthood of Christ After the order of Melchizedek Will accept only those kinds of Tithes; He identifies with the lost of the earth.

I believe Abraham and Melchizedek sat down at that communion table and Jesus began to proclaim that there would one day come another priesthood. Not a tithe, but a priesthood! It would be a priesthood that would accept the sin sickened lives of all the children by faith. This is why Abraham, the Father of Faith, of whose seed you are, was at the table. When, in the fullness of time, the Father would send forth His son, the Seed (Christ), planned from the foundations of the world. He will come and fulfill all that will be written in the law and the prophets.

When we get to Hebrews Chapter 7 you will see that the real issue was about the coming of another priesthood, not a tithe! It is not significant that Abraham paid tithes, but what is significant is that this priesthood accepted them. I assure you the entire message written in Hebrews Chapter 7 is about a priesthood that would come, Not a Tithe. What a wonderful High Priest we have. He is one who identifies with the filth of our lives and accepts us at the very point of redemption.

All of those born into the Body of Christ by faith are included in the promise of Father Abraham. God promised Abraham that he would have children who would exceed the number of the stars and the sand on the sea. We are those children of faith. Not born under the law, but made alive unto God, our Father, by faith alone. Whatsoever is not of faith is sin. Tithing is not of faith; it is of commandment and law. The law was added until that which was perfect came. (Jesus)

What amazes me the most is if you read this book looking for legal tithes or money, you will find it. That is all you will see! A heart trained on money or covetous practices will only see the natural every time.

Notice that Abraham gave a portion to three men: Aner, Eshcol, and Mamre. You must realize as these three men returned to their villages God was glorified and the God of Abraham was credited with the victory. This caused everyone to proclaim again, Abraham, surely you have the one true God.

Something worth mentioning is the picture of the evil king of Sodom as the enemy of the soul as he offers to let Abraham keep all of the goods. The king wanted only the people. The reality of this is a stark one. We must remember that the people who were living in Sodom had their hearts captured by substance and things. This city also had the lowest level of moral filth that would eventually cause God to destroy that city with fire. So captivating was its power and influence upon the soul that even Lot, Abraham's nephew, would return to that wicked city. However, one day there would eventually arise a priesthood that would possess the power to break even that power of Sodom and Gomorrah over the lives of His children.

Disobedience and covetousness, which is idolatry, keeps most from knowing the Master's Power over mammon today. Worldliness begins with justifying your personal abundance within your heart when you know there are those in need around you.

It is our heart cry to see Honor, Truth, Virtue,
Integrity, Holiness, and Righteousness
Restored to the Body of Christ.

If you are a religious tither let me encourage you to step from dead faith to find out for yourself if you can really hear Him. Is there any real difference between a church collecting tithes and a Sam's club or local VFW collecting dues from their members? Yes! At least at Sam's or the VFW you know what you get when you put your money down.

Wait until you see Abraham's Grandson Jacob's Tithing Habits in our next chapter. Jacob was the Second Tither in all of Scripture. You will not believe it! Get ready for A TEST on Jacob's Tithing Habits. **IF YOU UNDERSTAND JACOB THAT WILL BE ALL YOU NEED TO BE FREE FROM RELIGIOUS BONDAGE!**

The character of Abraham is amazing.

He chose not to touch even a shoelace. *He set an example, that many years later, others would follow. The Apostles, Sons of God, of the Promised Seed of Christ would remark as people came and laid money at their feet, "We will take none of it, but we will give ourselves to the Word, prayer, and fasting." My, how far we have fallen from real biblical faith.*

Jacob's Tithing Habits
"The Test"

Gen 28:20-22

20   Then Jacob made a vow, saying, "If God will be with me, and keep me in this way that I am going, and give me bread to eat and clothing to put on,

21   "so that I come back to my father's house in peace, then the LORD shall be my God.

22   "And this stone which I have set as a pillar shall be God's house, and of all that You give me I will surely give a tenth to You."(NKJ)

I am sure that everyone has experienced the tone that radiates from the television or the radio during a test of the emergency broadcast system. I suppose that annoying tone is better than hearing the words "Standby for an incoming missile." I would like to offer you "A Test" of the "Emergency Biblical Broadcast System." I am convinced by the LORD that this one example of Jacob's Tithing Habits has the ability to deliver you from the religious bondage of tithing forever. By answering just one question, "A Test" question, about Jacob's Tithing Habits you can walk away totally free. If you will think with me and will ask the Holy Spirit to grant you the spiritual eyes to see, this profound biblical truth will set you free.

Jesus said,
"You Shall Know the Truth, and Truth Shall Set You Free."

Unlike the annoying tone that we often hear during a test of the emergency broadcast system I ask you to listen for the pure undeniable Voice of Truth. That Voice of Truth has the power to deliver you from the incoming missile attack by the pulpit upon your faith and your wallet.

This is "A Test"
of the
Emergency Biblical
Broadcast System ...
Standby for Truth!
(As Paul Harvey would say.)

IN ALL OF YOUR CHURCH ATTENDANCE

How many times Have You Heard the Pulpit Expound on Jacob's Tithing Habits?

I am sure that most of you have heard your fair share of sermons on tithing by now. Please tell me the number of times that your pastor has preached on Jacob's Tithing Habits. The questions I ask you are very important. Stop and Really Think about them. <u>What, may I ask you, is the real reason the pulpit would skip Jacob?</u>

If we are to learn biblical tithing principles, then why has the pulpit failed to teach you about Jacob's tithing principles? All Scripture should interpret scripture on any given subject. Why haven't you heard as many messages on Jacob's tithing principles as you have heard on "Will a man rob God?" Why has the Loony Tune television network of TBN failed to frequently use Jacob's tithing habits to raise money? I ask the questions for a reason. Within them you will find the Voice of Truth. You, my friend, will believe a lie to be the truth until the lie is revealed to be one. Ever believe in Santa?

Jacob Is the Best Example of Tithing
In All of Scripture.
Then Why Would the Pulpit
Fail to Teach YOU about Jacob's Tithing Habits?

Just Look at Jacob's Qualifications!

In these passages of scripture we find Jacob, the grandson of Abraham, offering to pay God tithes. What better example can you find? <u>Jacob is The First Tither to put a 10 percent figure on the amount that he will personally give God.</u> Think about it. This is the man that God would eventually change his name from Jacob to Israel. Jacob would be the Father of the twelve tribes that would become the Nation Israel! What better or a more qualified individual can we find in scripture than this example of Jacob? <u>This man was the chosen patriarch by God to Birth the Entire Nation of Israel.</u>

He Was The Grandson of Abraham!

As the saying goes, "<u>It just doesn't get any better than this!</u>" Why would the leaders of our day Intentionally pass up this wonderfully qualified individual? Jacob appears by all accounts to be the best qualified man for the job. Jacob is the best example of personal tithing in all of scripture. I ask you to show me on one hand the number of times that you have heard a sermon on Jacob's Tithing Habits. Hold up just one finger if you can. I declare in spite of what you have not heard from the pulpit that Jacob's Tithing Habits are solid biblical foundational truth. Jacob's Tithing Habits will fully embrace every tithing principle in scripture from Genesis to Revelations. Why would the supposed men of God in this generation avoid teaching you about Jacob's Tithing Habits?

<u>Why does Jacob fail to fit into their tithing theology?</u>

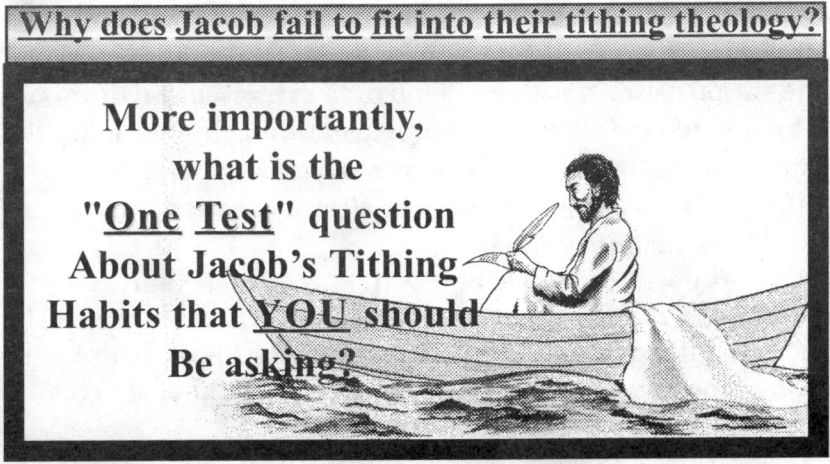

More importantly,
what is the
"<u>One Test</u>" question
About Jacob's Tithing
Habits that <u>YOU should</u>
Be asking?

Do You Realize ...That None Of Jacob's Tithing Habits Will "Fit" into a Single Sermon On Tithing That You Have Ever Heard.

I guarantee you that Jacob's Tithing Habits will not fit into a single sermon that you have heard about tithing. In fact, Jacob's actions will not fit into most sermons that you have heard on faith. Every biblical scholar knows that scripture is to interpret scripture. You cannot dismiss any part of scripture on a given subject in order to create our own theology. For anyone to Avoid the entire council of scripture on any given subject is the highest form of Pulpit Heresy! (Religious Treason!) The next time you hear a sermon on tithing I urge you to weigh its content with the knowledge of "Jacob's Tithing Habits."

Every tithing sermon is nothing more than manipulative coercion from the pulpit. The fruit of a tithing sermon is twofold. First of all it perverts true biblical faith. Secondly, the speaker uses it with one motive to extract money from the Children of God. This one example of tithing by Jacob has the power to destroy every sermon that you have ever heard on tithing. Jacob's example will also destroy about 90 percent of today's sermons on faith.

It does not matter how NICE you think your pastor is or what a great man of God he might be. I assure you IF he collects Tithes in any form, IF he justifies his existence with Tithe money he is in Error! Most are in intentional error by CHOICE! A Pulpit Heretic!

By now we are all familiar with the phrase, "If it doesn't fit you must acquit!" Biblical theology is the exact opposite of O.J.'s courtroom dilemma.

In biblical theology, every example on any given subject in scripture <u>MUST FIT</u> like a glove. For example, Jacob's Tithing Habits must fit every scripture about tithing in the Bible. In the courtroom of biblical theology we must say, "If it doesn't fit you <u>CANNOT</u> acquit!" For anyone to develop a doctrine or pulpit theology while intentionally avoiding a portion of scripture is a form of Spiritual Witchcraft. Everything you hear from the mouth of a prosperity preacher is Spiritual Witchcraft! Intentional deception originates from the birthplace of its father "The Deceiver."

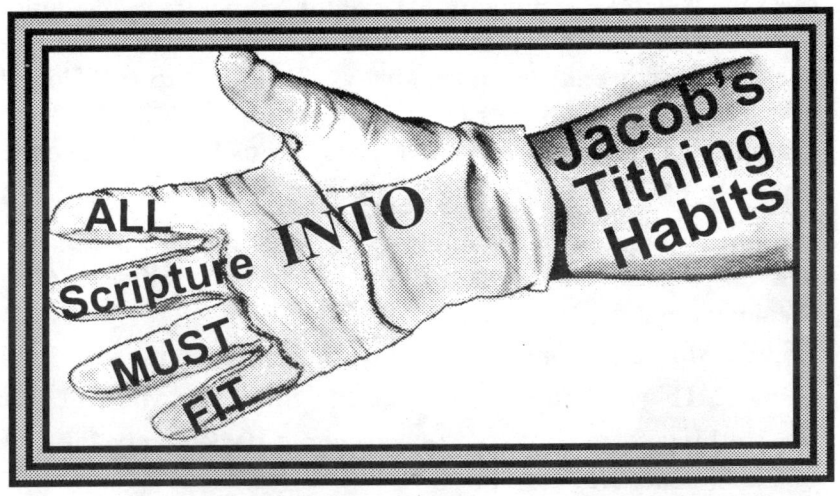

If the speaker does not include the principles found in Jacob's Tithing Habits into his sermon on tithing, then we must declare the speaker <u>GUILTY</u> of pulpit heresy! (Religious Treason and Spiritual Deception!) A real church will not preach about tithes or money. There are much greater issues to address within the body of Christ than the issues of carnal substances. Jacob's Tithing Habits and principles "Will Fit" into every biblical principle in scripture on tithing.

If you will seriously think with me, you will come to no other conclusion except GUILTY for the Emasculated Cheerleaders of our day! They intentionally fail to include all of scripture on tithing. In fact, their entire interpretation of what tithing was really about is off on every point.

Anyone that preaches tithing in the form of natural substance is in error. The word error is too kind for them; they intentionally deceive you. Some will claim they were ignorant of the facts. God does not bless massive intentional ignorance!

What happened to Paul's words of "Study to show yourself approved a good workman rightly dividing the word of truth?" The next time you hear a sermon about tithing make them put this glove on. If their message does not fit the principles that we will find in Jacob's Tithing Habits the message is heresy! (Religious Treason.) Ask yourself one more time. Why Haven't You Heard Sermons on How to Tithe like Jacob? Why are the sermons always, "Will a man rob God?" or "Seed Faith Giving," or perhaps as simple as "Can You Help Us Out?" There Are Several Reasons! Let's Examine Them.

THE FIRST REASON you will not hear a

sermon on Jacob's tithing habits is obvious. Jacob's manner of praying with words of doubt will not fit into today's pulpit theology on Tithes or Faith. Listen to him.

IF you will be with me … IF you will keep me in the way I am going … IF you will give me bread to eat … IF you will give me clothing to put on …IF I can come back to my father's house in peace …

That little word "If" poses too big of an obstacle for the pulpit. To the natural eye of the pulpit puppeteer there appears to be too much doubt and fear in Jacob's short request.

Jacob appears at this point in his prayer to be the biggest man of doubt in all of scripture. The If's are all there in Jacob's original statement. I added them above for personal emphasis on how this man prayed. We must also conclude that on the surface Jacob appears to be a man bound by tremendous fear.

Listen to the voice of fear. Will you be with me God? Will you keep me? Will you give me food? Will you give me clothes? How about a place to live? Will you keep me from troubles? Sound familiar? Who has not struggled with many of the same issues as Jacob?

Jacob appears to be the Oscar winner for the worst performance of faith in scripture. There is absolutely no way that any of Jacob's Tithing Habits and principles would fit into a single sermon on tithing today. The pulpit knows this. They also know that Jacob's Tithing Principles have the power to destroy every sermon that they have, or ever will preach about tithing. That is why you do not hear Jacob's Tithing Habits preached.

The "faithing" it crowd of positive confession would have to throw Jacob out of the back door of the church. To them Jacob does not know how to stand on the "Word of God" and claim his promises. I say Jacob knew God more intimately than all of them put together.

Jacob ... Would Say
To them and You.
YOU must LEARN
To Receive a Promise
Before
YOU can Claim One!

Jacob would say to them and you. You must learn to receive a promise before you can claim one! Faith comes by Hearing, not reading, quoting, or chanting the Word of God at God!

Jacob, in One Short "IF" Prayer, Causes the Entire Heretical ministry of Oral *C.* Roberts to Fall Powerless and Useless At His feet. Oral Cannot Establish One Word!

Some of you have had a pinch of that Copland/Hagin stuff stuck between your cheek and gums for so long that your mouth and life has become a cancerous obnoxious representation of Christ. Remember, "If Jacob's faith and tithing principles do not fit in their sermon you CANNOT acquit the HERETIC THAT SPEAKS FROM THE PULPIT!"

Jacob's Tithing Habits blows away the entire prosperity movement along with their doctrine of giving to get completely. Every sermon on faith by Kenneth Copland, Fred Price, Creflo Dollar, Oral Roberts, John Hagee, John Avanzini, Benny "Heretic" Hinn, Comedian Jesse Duplantis. and every other heretic that has appeared on TBN is also destroyed by Jacob's Tithing Habits. Every sermon you have ever heard from the mouth of "*Oral Cancer*" Roberts on Seed Faith is totally destroyed by Jacob. Jacob, in one short prayer, causes the entire ministry of "*Oral Cancer*" to fall powerless and useless at his feet. Oral cannot establish one word! Pick them up Oral and throw every word in the trash. While you are at it give Richard a broom also. You have polluted and littered Christianity with your mammonizing carnal words for too long. Your life is but vanity, and the shame of outer darkness awaits you.

The Father Of The "Seed Faith" Gospel!

The "Sons"

Satanic "Seed Faith" TRASH CREW

It is Time
To Take Out the Trash!

<u>Jacob is one of the strongest men of faith in all of scripture.</u> God chose Jacob to become the Patriarch and Father of the twelve tribes that would become the Nation Israel. I promise you there was nothing within Jacob that was faithless or fearful! As we shall see.

Can you imagine the audacity of any man demanding that God put up or shut up! God, <u>IF</u> you prove yourself to me first! Prove that you are real and then you can be my God! Basically, that is exactly what Jacob told God. I believe that there are very few today that would have Jacob's boldness and confidence to speak to God in this manner. Was this really what Jacob was saying? <u>IF</u> you will be with me, <u>IF</u> you'll keep me, <u>IF</u> you give me food, <u>IF</u> you give me clothing, <u>IF</u> you will let me go home in peace ... THEN THE LORD SHALL BE MY GOD!!

Jacob's Tithing Habits
As well as His Faith
Will <u>NOT FIT</u> into the Confines
Of Modern Pulpit Theology!

We Cannot Acquit Today's
Cheerleaders!
I Say They Are ...

GUILTY AS CHARGED

THE SECOND IMPORTANT REASON you
will not hear a sermon on Jacob's tithing principles is that it
would leave you, the tither, with a way out. The pulpit knows
that there are too many "If's" contained in Jacob's prayer that
would give you an excuse Not to Tithe! For instance, <u>What If</u>
you did not feel that God was with you? <u>What If</u> you felt that
God was not keeping you in the way you were going? <u>What If</u>
you ran into a hard time and found that food was scarce? <u>What
If</u> you were not getting clothing to put on? <u>What If</u> there was
trouble in your home and not peace? <u>What If</u> you lost your job
and could not pay your bills on time? According to Jacob,
would you have to tithe? No! The culprit in the pulpit knows
that there are too many possibilities that exist in Jacob's
Tithing Habits that would give you a reason <u>NOT</u> to tithe.

They figure why risk it. Why show you the If's? They
know "If You See" the IF's that would not be healthy for
keeping their <u>man made monetary illusion alive</u>. I would love
to be there to hear them scrambling and twisting scripture in
order to explain Jacob's tithing habits to you now. You can bet
that once this book is well circulated you will hear hundreds of
sermons on Jacob's Tithing Habits. Believe me, every one of
them will be another twisting perversion of the truth. The slick
Huxter will offer you a long Greek or Hebrew word study.
They will come up with every crafty scheme and bold remarks
about this book. None of them will ever be able to stand in my
presence before you, and publicly contradict the Spirit of
Truth.

> They have hidden the <u>IF'S</u> from you
> In **FEAR.**
> How foolish, the <u>IF'S</u> are not
> Important.

The reason they fear Jacob's If's is because their
original foundation about tithing is off the mark. To embrace
the truth at this point would expose too much error and
deception by them. Shame on Them! Jacob is much deeper and
more intimate with God, as we shall see in a moment.

Jacob clearly required that God perform everything before he would give God a tenth. The Burden of Proof Was Put on God! Prove yourself first God!

What is even more amazing about this entire incident is the fact that God took him up on it! Scripture bears that out. Maybe there was more to Jacob's Tithing Habits than you realize at this point. Your Father will always answer a prayer of Real Faith. Jacob got an answer to his supposed faithless, doubtful, fearful prayer that was filled with IF'S. Have you? **However, what is the more important "Test Question"** that you should be asking about **Jacob's Tithing Habits?**

My prayer is that the Holy Spirit will open your spiritual eyes and ears. Why cannot the leaders of our day preach or teach you about the beauty found in Jacob's tithing habits and principles? It is because their eyes are trained on covetous carnal things. They are out of communion with the Spirit of Truth and can only observe Jacob's Tithing Habits with the natural eyes from a soul filled with desires of the flesh. They read about Jacob's Tithing Habits with a heart of fear. Fear that you will find out the truth. They are afraid that you will question the IF'S contained in Jacob's prayer.

The IF'S are Irrelevant!

What and whom you may think are Great Men of God in our day actually have more fear and doubt than Jacob ever did. Jacob had none! Again, what is the <u>One Test Question</u> about Jacob's Tithing Habits that YOU should be asking?

Was Jacob Really Full of Doubt?
Was He Really Full of Fear?
A Thousand Times No!

Jacob's If's were not doubt. The bondage and fear of possessing natural substance did not trap Jacob. He was not weak in his faith. Jacob, like everyone, was looking for a deeper reality of God in his life. That reality is only found within the chambers of your heart. I hope that your reality of God within your own life is not based upon the possession of natural things. As a parent, you have the responsibility to point your children towards God. Your children can and will observe your example of serving God from your life.

However, there will come a time in their lives when they must know God for themselves. Jacob was at the same crossroads that his Father Isaac and his Grandfather Abraham had come to many times in their own lives. Jacob was about to enter a deeper more intimate relationship with God than he had ever had before.

Imagine knowing God as intimately as Abraham did. Abraham knew God well enough to take his promised son Isaac and willingly offer him to God as a living sacrifice. (Genesis Chapter 22). I venture to say if anyone heard that request from God today we would attribute the voice to be the very voice of the devil himself. Imagine Abraham's heart and the flood of emotions that he faced as he took Isaac and tied him to the altar. Think of the tremendous terror and the emotions that Isaac must have encountered as his Father Abraham raised the knife to kill him.

On their way up the mountain Isaac questioned his Father Abraham, " Father, where is the lamb for the sacrifice?" Abraham's comment was, "The Lord will provide the lamb for the sacrifice." It was not until Abraham had lifted the knife to kill his own son that God stopped him and provided a sacrifice.   Surely, You Do Not Believe That Jacob Never Heard That Story as he grew up.

Many of us think we know God intimately. Do you? Many think they know God as provider, ... do you really? The issue with God will always be intimate trusting faith in a deep relationship with Him.   To imply that the creator of the universe needs your money to keep the church doors open, or that God needs your money to reach the lost, is blasphemous to a Sovereign Holy God.   Abraham knew God way past God's sovereignty over the natural substance of things in his life. Have you traded that intimacy for the cruel bondage inherited from the law of tithing?

Jacob realized that to have a Genuine Reality of God he would have to recognize God as the only sovereign source of all substance in his life. He would also have to forfeit control of his own life along with the acceptance of that recognition.   The possession of that reality is not a cheap one.

It also means you must accept whatever <u>LEVEL OF LIFE</u> God determines you to have. I will give you a tenth God, open my eyes and heart to accept the Reality of your Sovereign Provision within my Life right where I am at this moment was Jacob's prayer. Is that yours? Are you content with all things? Tithing is not the issue. <u>**Giving God a tenth of what he has given you is nothing more than the pointless shuffling of money by you. Religious flesh at work!**</u> Are you still foolish enough to think you can offer God anything? How many "If's" have your lips uttered in your search to find a tangible intimate reality of God in your life?   I am sure that many of you will say and actually believe that you know God as your Source. Then why do you tithe?

Nevertheless, I can hear some of you say
Jacob still paid tithes!
Did He? Are You Sure?

What Is the ONE "TEST QUESTION"
About Jacob's Tithing Habits
That You Should Be Asking?
Are You Ready?

When we looked at tithing under the Levitical priesthood of the law, we found that the tither ate the tithe. We also found that Abraham had a meal of bread and wine with Melchizedek. The tithes that Abraham gave to Melchizedek did not come from the strength of his own hand. Abraham did not take one thin dime out of his pocket and drop it in Melchizedek's basket. Abraham clearly proclaimed that it was God who had given him the victory. Abraham knew God as the Sovereign Source of all things natural and supernatural within his life. In both examples, tithing under the law and Abraham, we found that tithing was about Communion with the Father.

Jacob Promised
To Give God a Tenth.
Are You Ready?
Here Is the One Test Question
That You
Should Have Asked!

"The Test" Question

ABOUT JACOB'S TITHING HABITS IS:

Where Was Jacob Going to Pay His Tithe?

There was no Synagogue or Temple. There was not a Levitical priesthood. Moses was a long way from being born. God had not given the law yet.

So where and how was Jacob going to pay his tithes? If tithing was about money Jacob had a real problem at this point. Was he going to throw the 10 percent he promised God on the rock? How was Jacob going to give God a tenth? Was God going to send down an offering plate weekly? Maybe Jacob was going to just throw the Tithe up into the air.

TITHING IS NOT ABOUT MONEY!

Jacob's Tithing Habits will Fit
Every Biblical Scripture and Principle on Tithing!

Just Like a Glove!

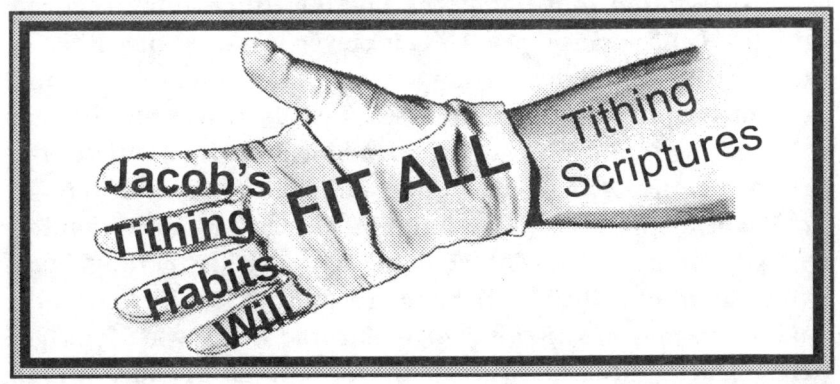

The First Principle We Found in Our Study on Tithing.
(The tithe was eaten by the tither.)

Under the law, the tither ate the tithe recognizing that God was the only sovereign source of all substance in their lives. Jacob's If's are not doubts. God did not chastise Jacob for using the word "IF" in his prayer! Just as his Grandfather Abraham had lifted his hand to God saying, "I will take nothing not even a shoelace" from the spoils of war. Abraham gave nothing to Melchizedek that came from the strength of his own hand. Jacob's prayer openly recognizes that nothing, NOT EVEN A TENTH ... can come into his life by his own strength. GOD WOULD HAVE TO PROVIDE HIS OWN TENTH FOR JACOB TO TITHE! Who is the man that says he can add one thing to God's account? Where is the man that can uphold God? Show me the man that can give God anything that God did not first give to that man! Abraham, Jacob, and the Tither under the Law recognized God as the only Sovereign Source of all Substance in their lives. You may say that you recognize God as your source in your head ... but do you possess an intimate heart Reality of this? Is it visible in your Life? It will cost you everything! Do you Hear Him?

The Second Principle We Have Found in Our Study on Tithing. (Tithing was to be only on the increase.)

We found that under the law the tither only practiced tithing on an increasing scale. God never required the tither to tithe anything on a decreasing scale. There is not one account in all of scripture where anyone was ever instructed to tithe on a decreasing scale. This second principle only substantiates the first principle. It is God's responsibility to produce sovereign provision in the life of His children. God desires communion within your heart. Even Jacob recognized this truth. If you will do all of this, then I will have the ability to give you a tenth. Godly Graciousness is birthed within the heart when you get here. Jacob also knew that tithing would be only on an increasing scale. How else would Jacob be able to pay a tithe unless there was an increase? More important is the question of how and where would Jacob pay his tithe?

The Third Principle We Have Found in Our Study on Tithing. (Tithing was directly between the tither and God.)

Tithing was always directly between the tither and God. Under the law, the tither ate a meal in the presence of God. There was no middleman. Abraham directly gave tithes of the spoils of war to Melchizedek, a type of Christ. Jacob agreed to directly give God a tenth. How was he going to do that? Remember that there was No Temple or synagogue. God had not given the law yet. Jacob fulfills every tithing scripture and principle thus far in our study. Jacob understood that tithing would be a personal intimate reality between him and God alone. Do you know God intimately enough to pray as boldly as Jacob prayed? Do you pray out of desperation? A broken and contrite heart He will not turn away. Learn how to pray out of preparation.

HOW AND WHERE WAS JACOB GOING TO PAY HIS TITHE?

The <u>Fourth</u> <u>Principle</u> We Have Found in Our Study on Tithing. (Give to those in need around you.)

Under the law, we found that the tither emptied his barns and storehouses in the third year and gave the excess to the strangers, orphans, and widows within his gates. This act of faith kept the tither totally dependent upon God as his sovereign source. As the children of God became a blessing to those around them, God received glory unto Himself. Imagine someone emptying their bank account just to feed you. Then over time you would witness their God fill their accounts up again. By this generous act of kindness being expressed through the lives of God's children He received much glory! The receiver of such blessings could but proclaim, "Surely you have the one true God!" In the same manner, Abraham gave a portion from the spoils of war to those who were with him. As they returned to their villages everyone had to proclaim that surely Abraham had the one true God. If there is one thing that the church desperately needs, it would be the Wisdom of Understanding the Glory of God.

So Where and How Did Jacob Pay His Tithes?

Jacob did the same thing that his Father Isaac and Grandfather Abraham had done. Jacob gave his tithe to the strangers, widows, and orphans. Tithing is about communion with your Father. <u>Tithing ... Is Not</u> about dropping money in a basket because you heard a good message. <u>Tithing ... Is Not</u> about church attendance or building programs. <u>Tithing ... Is Not</u> about keeping your account with God paid up! <u>Tithing ... Is Not</u> about a denomination. <u>Tithing ... Is Not</u> about keeping your religious institution alive. <u>Tithing ... Is Not</u> about paying your local Heretic a $alary! If he collects tithes from you his Doctrine does not "<u>FIT</u>" Jacob's Tithing Habits!

Therefore, <u>You Cannot</u> Acquit!

Tithing Is about Intimate Communion with Your Father. Tithing Is about Hearing God!

Tithing Is the Recognition By You That God Is the Only Sovereign Source of Provision in Your Life.

Tithing Is Allowing God To Express Himself Through Your Life To Those Around You In Need.

People will never know your God based on your words or your altar calls. People will not see God because of the size of your church membership. They will not see God because of your knowledge of the Bible. They will know God and see Him when you know God enough to hear Him and touch the lives of those around you in humility. Jacob was not arrogant, doubtful, or fearful. Jacob knew God intimately enough to be honest about the reality of God in his life. He forfeited his selfish pride for the same intimate humility his father and grandfather possessed. Aren't you tired of religion? Remember that God took Jacob up on his offer filled with "If's." Try it, it sure beats pew sitting. Let God show You who He wants to Bless through You Life. Give Him The Glory!

I would not do you justice if I did not mention Jacob's vow. Years ago televangelist Robert Tilton was taking in approximately 80 million dollars a year using the scam of making a vow to God. **Jacob's vow speaks of his seriousness with God and nothing more. It Was Not Your Vow. It is NOT a vow to be used on you.**

While it is in the book and we can find truth contained in these scriptures remember it was Jacob's vow of 10% to God. Not Yours! Jacob was BEFORE The Law!

I personally have made many vows to God in my lifetime. As a lost fisherman I used to always try to cut a deal with God over a large mouth bass. "If you will let me catch the world record bass I will split the money with you." I never caught the bass, God hooked me, and Robert Tilton hooked many innocent people. It is a shame that the body of Christ (YOU) would tolerate anyone like Robert Tilton. It is time for you to stand up and speak out against such blasphemous UN-Christ like wolves in sheep's clothing. This is not a day to remain silent. The next time you hear another sermon on tithing, make the culprit in the pulpit take The Tithing Challenge and Put the Glove on!

Remember if Jacob's Tithing Habits and the tithing principles that we have studied "Do Not Fit," YOU CANNOT acquit the speaker! He is guilty of Religious Treason and spiritual deception! A Pulpit Heretic!

Before we go to the famous passages of Malachi Chapter 3, "Will a man rob God?" I feel it will be necessary to stop at another passage scripture that is used frequently by the pulpit and televangelists. The passages in the next chapter have nothing to do with tithing and everything to do with giving to get seed faith mentality. Every telethon will use the prophet Elijah and the widow woman as a cornerstone in their fund-raising schemes. Every heretic with a prosperity message will feed you Elijah and the widow woman, until you choke on their intentional deceptive religious treason.

This has been "A Test" Of The Emergency Biblical Broadcast System. Be Free!

Elijah and the Widow Woman of Zarephath.
First Kings Chapter 17: 8-16

This one story has been used more than any other passage of scripture to raise money. Every telethon on TBN will have some televangelist perverting and twisting the truths from this beautiful story of Faith. Pulpits that preach Prosperity instead of Reality use these passages to extract money from those who are in need themselves. These passages are the cornerstone of the giving to get "Seed Faith" gospel that we here today. While they have little to do with tithing, I felt it necessary to address the lies that you may have heard about these passages. It will help unravel tons of false doctrine found among the charismatic fanatics. It never ceases to amaze me how many people are coerced and manipulated into giving out of their need by these Vultures. Like vultures picking at a dead carcass, they use these passages to extract money, vows, tithes, and "Seed Faith" giving from those in need. As Masters of deception, they knowingly rob the poor for their own benefit.

If you have ever heard a sermon on Elijah and the widow woman of Zarephath, I ask you to compare the truth found in these passages against what you have heard. If you will take the time to think about the naked truth in these scriptures, another prosperity preacher will never be able to deceive you again. We will pull the mask off the Old Lone Ranger by the time we are finished. I am also going to tug on Superman's Cape … I found out these men are not Superman. They are not from God at all!

Every doctrine in the prosperity, positive confession, giving to get gospel will fall powerless before the Voice of Truth! By the time we are finished I think Oral Roberts will have to give the rest of the prosperity preachers a broom and dustpan.

In an upcoming book WHO ARE THESE MEN? I will scripturally expose every one of these men. They are in the book! They are a clear biblical indicator of what day and hour we are living in.

The only truth I have observed about Oral Roberts is the prophetic correctness of his first name. He is an "*Oral Blasphemous Cancer*" to the integrity of the Body of Christ. I would be unkind if I did not compliment Oral's ability to Clone Himself in his son Richard. We know every tree will bear fruit after the order of its kind. One can observe Richard and all you can think is … **What Is It**? Richard's life is completely unable to cast its own shadow. What a shame that is!

Take this time to think. What I ask you to do is examine the truth of what really took place between Elijah and the widow woman. If you will do this, I promise you will never be able to listen to another prosperity preacher! Unless, of course, you continue to deny the truth like they do. Many of you that are involved in the prosperity movement do so because of an internal weakness. Flesh begets Flesh! A prosperity preacher can only appeal to a living internal ungodly carnal desire that resides within your heart. I urge you to get the video series on Lordship. If it does not produce a deeper reality of Christ in you and help deliver you from the snare of the Fowler, I will give you a full refund. You have nothing to lose and everything to gain. As we study these passages we will not read anything into them.

They will stand on the strength of the Visible Truth that is contained within them. Truth is sustained by His own power. No man has the ability to uphold truth. The source of All Truth is His own Entity.

> **Truth is Sustained By His own Power. No man Has the ability To uphold Truth. The source Of All Truth is … His own Entity.**

The worst interpretation I have ever heard on these passages was by John Avanzini. During a TBN fundraiser John Avanzini gave a dissertation about Elijah and the widow woman that went something like this. You see child of God what you need to do is trust the man of God with your financial statement. The first thing Elijah did when he arrived was to take a financial assessment of the widow woman's situation. If the widow woman withheld her financial condition from the man of God, she would not have received the blessing. You see, what some of you need to do is to take your financial conditions and turn them over to the man of God. You need to turn over your bank statement to the man of God. If you can't trust the man of God, why who you gonna trust child of God? Some of you need to pick up the phone and call right now with a pledge OUT OF YOUR NEED. Some of you need to turn over your finances to your pastor. Wake up child of God, you can't out give God. "Oh glory," shouted Jan and Paul Crouch. Mascara running and a handkerchief wiping her false tears of joy Jan said, "What a Word." I Say What a Crock!

Blah ... Blah ... Blah!
Aren't You Sick of Such Foolish Blasphemous Heresy!
Is It Any Wonder
The Lost Think That We Have Lost Our Minds?

Those possessed with a natural heart and eye will only speak of natural things. Every message that you hear from the mouths of charlatans like *"Oral Cancer Roberts"* and John Avanzini will always have a perspective of God relational to natural substances. Their hearts speak for their Master ... Mammon! God is a spirit and those that worship Him must worship Him in Spirit and Truth! No one has ever left this planet with one dollar. I have yet to see a hearse with a U-Haul behind it. Every preacher living a lavish life with his hand stuck out collecting Tithe money from the children of God is a thief and a robber of the True Faith of Christ.

These men are not in the book. I take that back. Yes, they are, but they are certainly not among the Men of God we read about in scripture. They are numbered amongst the Simons, Ahabs, Judas', and Jezebels in the book. Examine with me to the Simple Truths in scripture of what really took place between Elijah and the widow woman.
Be free!

I Kings 17:8-9

8   Then the word of the LORD came to him, saying,
9   "Arise, go to Zarephath, which belongs to Sidon, and dwell there. <u>See, I have commanded a widow there to provide for you."</u>
(NKJ)

From the very beginning, it is obvious that God told Elijah to go to Zarephath. It is also evident that God had already spoken to the widow woman. The passage clearly says, "I have commanded a widow there to provide for you." Elijah went to Zarephath with the knowledge that God had already spoken to a widow woman and she was commanded by God to take care of him. From the very beginning of the story you can throw away every lie you have heard about these passages. Better yet, just throw it on the floor. "<u>Oral Cancer Roberts</u>" will sweep it up! This story is not one of ignorance on the part of Elijah or the widow woman. Real Biblical Faith is not spiritual mysticism, hype, or guesswork. Faith is not blind ignorance or guesswork in action. Faith is hearing and obeying God. **The prophet Elijah went to Zarephath knowing there would be a widow woman there that had also been in touch with God.**

R E A D

IKings 17:10-11

10   So he arose and went to Zarephath. And when he came to the gate of the city, **INDEED** a widow was there gathering sticks. And he called to her and said, "Please bring me a little water in a cup, that I may drink."
11   And as she was going to get it, he called to her and said, "Please bring me a morsel of bread in your hand."

R E A D

Simplicity says when Elijah arrived everything was just as God said it would be. **Indeed** there was a widow woman there. I suppose a widow woman may have worn a certain type of clothing. Maybe that is how he recognized her. Some of you may search that out. What is important is the fact that Elijah immediately recognized the widow woman. Because she was at the gate gathering sticks, it was obvious she was preparing to cook something. God did not tell Elijah to go to the city and figure out which widow woman he was looking for. Faith is not guesswork! God had the widow woman at the gate gathering sticks to cook a meal. We cannot dismiss the fact that the widow woman was also there for a reason. She was at the gate looking for the man of God that she had been commanded by God to sustain. If you are familiar with Elijah's ministry as a prophet of God, you know that Elijah had prophesied a drought upon the lands. The situation had put water and food in a short supply. Elijah knew that God was going to provide for him through this widow woman. "See, I have commanded a widow there to provide for you."

> ## The widow woman knew Elijah was coming.
> ## She was at the gate looking for him.

I Kings 17:12-14

12   So she said, "As the LORD your God lives, I do not have bread, only a handful of flour in a bin, and a little oil in a jar; and see, I am gathering a couple of sticks that I may go in and prepare it for myself and my son, that we may eat it, and die."

13   And Elijah said to her, **"Do not fear;** go and do as you have said, but make me a small cake from it first, and bring it to me; and afterward make some for yourself and your son.

14   **"For thus says the LORD God of Israel**: 'The bin of flour shall not be used up, nor shall the jar of oil run dry, until the day the LORD sends rain on the earth.'"(NKJ)

"For thus says The LORD God Of Israel."

Elijah did not take a forty minute break between the words "make me a cake and thus says the Lord God." The widow woman's answer was not a desperate one. The way she answered Elijah tells a lot. When Elijah asked her for a morsel of bread she responded, <u>**"As the Lord your God lives."**</u> She could just as easily have said, **"I know who you are." "You are Elijah the prophet!" "You are the one that God commanded me to sustain."**

I do not believe that there were many around in those days that did not know who Elijah was. <u>Remember God had commanded her concerning Elijah.</u>  In verse 9 God had told Elijah "See, I have commanded a widow there to provide for You." To assume that the widow woman was kept in ignorance by God is foolishness. She knew who was coming. I believe God told her I am sending you my Prophet Elijah. When you hear him say, <u>"For thus says the Lord God of Israel,"</u> do whatever he says and I will sustain him and you. It is not presumptuous on my part or anyone's to assume that God had fully informed the widow woman as to who was coming. WHEN SHE HEARD <u>"For thus says the Lord God of Israel:"</u>

IKings 17:14-16

15   So she went away and did according to the word of Elijah; and she and he and her household ate for many days.
16   The bin of flour was not used up, nor did the jar of oil run dry, according to the word of the LORD which He spoke by Elijah.(NKJ)

The widow woman did nothing until she heard the words, "For thus says the Lord God of Israel." It should be evident to you that this woman operated only on a spoken word of God from the mouth of His prophet. As soon as she heard, "For thus says the Lord," she went away and did what Elijah told her to do. Verse 16 is clear on the fact that it was the spoken word of God through the mouth of this prophet Elijah that <u>sustained</u> them.

The next time you hear someone twisting and perverting the pure faith of the widow woman and her childlike reliance on the spoken word of God, stand up. Do not just sit there; it is time for you to take a stand.

If the speaker claims to be a prophet and is collecting money, all of church history proves he is a false prophet! Prophets are never in it for the money. In fact, prophets are not involved by choice; it is by God's design and divine election! You will never find a Real Prophet of God with his hand stuck out for money saying, "Can you help me get the gospel out?" "If you like this ministry send in your donations." "We need your help to stay on the air." When you hear any statements appealing for money it is time for you to take a stand. Your silence only condones their behavior. When you stand, speak out!

If you want to be politically correct tell the heretic, "Elijah I know and Elisha I know ... and preacher you are neither!" If you will begin to perform a little "*Oral*" Surgery right where you are things will begin to change. It is not a day to remain silent. Your Silence Condones Their Blasphemous Unholy Behavior! Call In and Complain during a TBN Sheep Fleecing, Mammonizing, Fund-Raising Telethon. CALL REPEATEDLY!

The widow woman waited at the city gate for the prophet of God. She knew God well enough to recognize His voice. The remarkable level of faith that was demonstrated by her is astounding. She demonstrates the simplicity of faith that God requires those who call upon Him to walk in. Without faith it is impossible to please God. FAITH COMES BY HEARING! It was the spoken word of God through the mouth of His prophet Elijah that *SUSTAINED* them.

The story was not about the preacher getting something from a widow woman first or was it about her ability to give the prophet of God a statement of her financial condition!

There is a place prepared for
John Avanzini!
It does not Slumber,
He will give account!

The widow woman and Elijah are a clear demonstration of simple faith in action. That precious widow woman on the very edge of life found herself sustained by one thing ... **A** **Real** **Word** **from** **God**. Today, many use a slang term in Christian theological circles proclaiming themselves to be on "The Cutting-Edge" of a move of God. Blah ... blah ... blah! This widow woman is a genuine example of someone REALLY on the cutting edge of a move of God.

Elijah and the widow woman did not go out and buy a gold plated chariot. New and fancy clothing never filled their closets. Elijah did not need a Lear jet for his ministry. There is no record of them shouting and jumping up and down claiming the Word of God as their divine right to "inherited promises." By faith they did not build another story on top of her house claiming that the blessings of God were with them. They did not speak things into existence with haughtiness.

NO, THEY ATE THEIR BREAD IN HUMILITY and thankfulness before God. They did this as they watched the famine reek havoc on the lives of those around them. That famine was also a word from God spoken through the mouth of His Prophet Elijah. They lived like that for over three years watching death and knowing that God had preserved them. It was three years before Elijah received another word from God to bring rain and end the famine. THERE IS A FAMINE IN THE EARTH TODAY AND IT IS FOR A REAL WORD FROM GOD.

As I write I must fight back the tears. My heart is heavy and my soul aches within me. Sorrowful Anger is present with me. I am filled with the fire of God within my soul at what they have done to the house of my King!

The impending judgment of God that awaits them also overwhelms me. I will not rest, I will not shut up, nor will I sit down. I will not forfeit Godly Discernment to the fear of offending them. May you choose to Stand. Fear God more than the Heretic if you have become enlightened by the Holy Spirit. Silence serves no one but the enemy of the Cross!

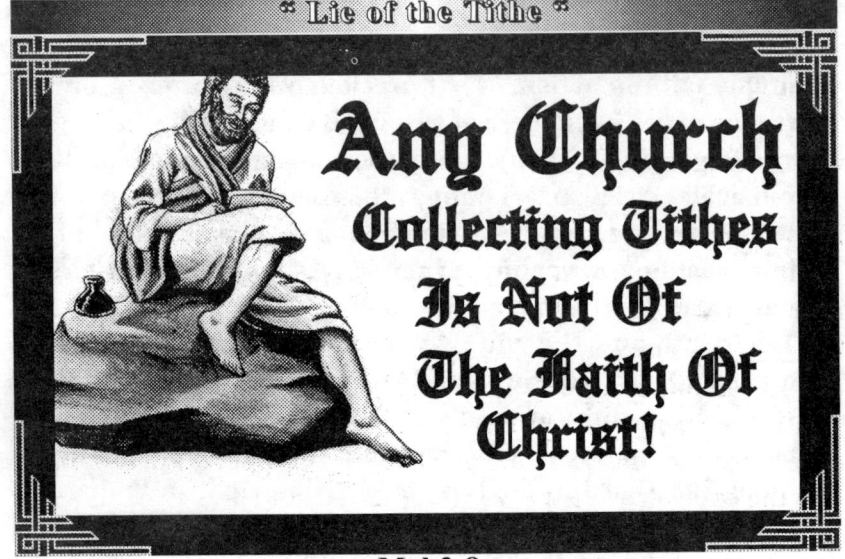

Mal 3:8

"Will a man rob God?" Yet you have robbed Me!
But you say, 'In what way have we robbed You?' In
tithes and offerings.(NKJ)

Who Was God Speaking To?

A Study in the Law ... To Catch a Thief!

I hope that by now the often-used scriptures from
Malachi Chapter 3 do not sound as intimidating to you as they
did before you started reading this book. At this point I am
going to devote more space to this passage. Not because it is
difficult. I regret that it will be necessary to spend a lot of time
here. However, I feel we must. This will be necessary because
of the numerous twisted perversions that have been rendered
by the pulpit on these passages. *I urge you* to take your time
and really think with me as we look at the **Grave
Intentional Errors** that have been committed by the
pulpit. Read every verse! By now you should realize that
something is seriously wrong with the INSTITUTIONALIZED
Church and its collection of money from the Children of God.

Not one sermon about tithing that was preached to you from Malachi Chapter 3 has been truthful or correct if the speaker was about to take an offering. Even more disturbing is this fact. The majority of every sermon that you have heard on tithing has been intentionally preached to you in error. Every sermon that you have heard on tithing from the pulpit must be thrown away as Irrelevant trash. Just put it in the trash can ... over there, ... you know, ... the one that "*Oral*" is holding.

In our study on tithing we have found that the pulpit has failed on every point to interpret scripture correctly. As I said the improper interpretation, for the most part, is intentional by the speaker.

I do not care who he is, if he preaches the Law of Tithing, he does it for one purpose. Money! It does not matter who it is. From the Pope to Billy Graham, if they preach tithing, they do it in Intentional Error!

Think about it. These men are supposed to be Christian leaders. They are to study the scriptures, pray, and hear from God. Do they stand and speak publicly in the name of God? Do they profess that they are God's servants? Then, why would God have failed to show them the real issues involved in tithing that we have seen? **GOD DIDN'T!**

Tell anyone of them from the Pope to Charles Stanley at First Baptist in Atlanta. If they speak publicly in the name of God, then let's have them open the book publicly and prove their doctrine on tithing. I will come and stand before them. Let them publicly prove to you in my presence that they have a right to collect money from you in the form of tithes and/or offerings according to the law. Let them prove that they are not Robbing You of an Intimate Relationship with your Father based on Faith! Don't hold your breath, the last thing that they want to do is stand in my presence and publicly open the book and debate in front of you. They will do a lot of talking to you without me there. They will offer a thousand explanations why you should continue to tithe. Why would they continue to LIE to you? More than tithing is at issue.

They know that They will have to prove that you are not sitting in <u>THEIR</u> Man Made Illusion if I am there. The exposure of their shallow faith is too risky for them. How can they justify collecting tithes after the law? *If they cannot prove their right to collect tithes in the form of money, then we must declare what they have built is of their*

OWN FLESH!

Their lives were supposed to lead you by example. They were to be a Living Epistle of how you were to live by Faith in Christ.

Leaders? Nay!
Emasculated Cheerleaders?
Yes!

A Brief "<u>Common</u> <u>Sense</u>" Study
In the Law

Let's examine some common sense questions about the law before we proceed in our study. I would like to ask you some questions concerning the law. Questions, that perhaps, you should have asked yourself a long time ago. Some of these questions have probably been in your heart anyway. Think on them carefully.

1. Why would a New Testament church use an Old Testament Law in order to extract money from its members? Why call it a New Testament church if it practices Old Testament Law? Is there any difference between the Old Testament Temple and the New Testament Church? If your pastor uses the Law of Tithing to raise money so that he can keep the church doors open, <u>IS</u> <u>THAT</u> <u>CHURCH</u> <u>REALLY</u> <u>BUILT</u> <u>ON</u> <u>FAITH</u>?

2. <u>With</u> <u>all</u> <u>of</u> <u>the</u> <u>laws</u> <u>that</u> <u>are</u> <u>contained</u> <u>in</u> <u>the</u> <u>Old</u> <u>Testament,</u>

WHY IS THIS LAW OF TITHING THE <u>ONLY</u> PHYSICAL <u>LAW</u>
That is practiced by the New Testament church of today?

In our study we have found that their interpretation is in error. Why is that? With all of the time for personal studying, how did they miss the simple fact that the Tither Ate the Tithe? The obvious conclusion is that the practice of this Law is Intentional on their part. Why?

3. Why doesn't your pastor follow the Ceremonial Washings, Circumcision, and Animal Sacrifice that are also contained in the law? With all of the ordinances and commands that are in the law, **why do you suppose** this Law of Tithing is the only law that the pulpit embraces?

Do you really believe that God needs your money to get the Gospel out or to do what you might call good works on the earth?

Under the Law
God Had a Law Library!

Think with me. Let's suppose that God wanted a Law Library for us to study from. If you have ever visited a Christian bookstore you are aware that today we have a book on everything. Go to your local Christian bookstore and just look around. Suppose that the same individuals who wrote the books in the bookstore were each commissioned by God to write a book on just one law, ordinance, or command in the Old Testament. In the end, I am sure God would have a rather large library on the law. Perhaps many of today's writers would also try to impress us with their Greek and Hebrew knowledge. Maybe your pastor has impressed you with his knowledge of Greek and Hebrew words. Ask yourself, how can they study so much and miss the Simple Truths that we have found in our study?

I assure you that I have studied every Greek and Hebrew word relational to this subject. However, I find that it is more important to speak in a common sense manner of Simple Truth to you. I would rather speak one word of Truth from the Heart to you, than a 10,000-word dissertation of head knowledge.

The priest and everyone that worked in the temple studied the law every day. Errors performed by the High Priest would and did result in death. If that does not make you serious about studying, I do not know what will.

Every ordinance by the Levitical priesthood was kept after the ___Natural Observance___ of things.

Sadly, they missed the internal heart of the matter. I can assure you that the Law Library that God established was followed to perfection by the High Priest in most cases. Not one natural law was left unobserved by him. Otherwise, when he entered the holy of holies annually, death awaited him.

Every day he carefully scrutinized and meditated on every law. We must say one thing about the Levitical priesthood. They studied the laws of God intensely. We cannot charge them with dereliction of duty in their knowledge of the law.

> **Every book in God's Law Library**
> **Was completely used by them!**
> **Not one book was left UN-turned.**

By the time Jesus arrived, the law had become their God as well as their identity. They had taken the law to the extreme level of nat straining and camel swallowing. The Levitical priesthood was corrupt on many occasions. Historically, we know there was repeated corruption in both the priesthood as well as the nation Israel. They fell away from God repeatedly all throughout the Old Testament. Nevertheless, the priesthood had taken the Law Library of God very seriously.

Corrupt or Not, They Used

EVERY

Book in the Law Library And observed

EVERY

Natural Law.

Now come forward with me about 2000 years. Suppose that the same Law Library existed today. Let's say that our Law Library was commissioned by God to be written by the individuals who have books in the Christian bookstore. I think we would have a fair sized library. Imagine the preachers of this generation going into the Law Library and checking out only one book. <u>Week after week, all they would repeatedly do is check out the same book.</u> Every other book within our Law library did but one thing ... collect dust! Why would our Law Library only have one book checked out each week by the *supposed* men of God? You must realize that this is exactly what your pastor does. He reaches into the Law Library and only observes and practices One Natural Law upon you week after week.

He will not check out the book on Circumcision. Has he ever publicly circumcised anyone on the eighth day after the birth of a child? He has not checked out the book on Ceremonial Washings. Has he publicly performed the ceremonial washings of the priesthood before getting dressed to preach? No! He will, however continue to check out only one book from the Law Library. That book is the Natural Law on Tithing and HE WILL NOT APPLY THAT BOOK TO HIMSELF. He cannot if he eats from the offering plate containing your tithes. HE PUTS NOTHING INTO THE PLATE THAT HE DID NOT FIRST TAKE OUT OF THE PLATE THE WEEK BEFORE. Therefore, the natural law that he preaches to you does not get applied to himself. However, he will continue to apply that one natural law to <u>YOU</u> week after week!

If you do not have an altar full of continual fire in the middle of your church, then your pastor has failed to check out the law book on altars and fire. Is he offering upon the altar a blood sacrifice? Has he slit the throat of a sheep in the doorway of your church?

Have you observed Your Pastor inspecting the sacrifice for external blemishes? Have you seen him inspecting the internal intestines for tumors and perfection?

Welcome to the First
Institutionalized Church
Where We Practice Some
Of the Law Some of the time.
(Barf or What?)

Practice All Of
The Law

FILTHY
IMPERFECTIONS
UNCLEAN

I speak this way to expose their foolishness and greed. He will tell you to accept Christ's Total Sacrifice for payment of Sin According to the Law. He will tell you that Christ fulfilled all of the requirements of a Holy God Under the Law. However, he will not build an altar and offer up a blood sacrifice. He will not observe ANY other natural law.

He will, however, continue to intentionally observe the Tithing Law. <u>Something is wrong with their Contradictory Theology.</u> I hope that you will begin to see and hear their overwhelming contradictory statements from the pulpit.

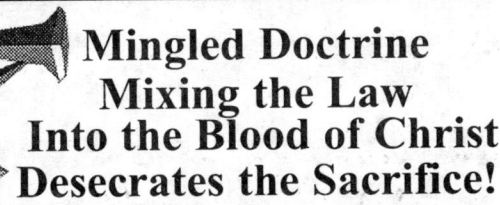

**Mingled Doctrine
Mixing the Law
Into the Blood of Christ
Desecrates the Sacrifice!**

Listen to the Voice of Mingled Contradiction and Hypocrisy. Your pastor will proclaim that the Kingdom of God is within you. He will tell you that if you have been born again by the Holy Spirit, you have the Holy Spirit residing within you. (I wonder what or who resides in them.) Your pastor will teach you that you are the righteousness of God in Christ Jesus. He will tell you there is nothing you can do in the Natural Strength of your flesh to Earn your salvation. He will tell you that salvation is a free gift from God. He will speak about the wonderful liberties that you have in Christ. He will talk about the tender mercies and the promises of God. You will hear about the Grace of God that passes human understanding! He will tell you that God loves you.

You will hear about the handwriting of ordinances that were against you as a sinner. You will also hear how Christ and his atonement wiped them out. If he is good, he will tell you the Law was given to Moses.

If he is better than good he will also tell you that the Law was <u>ISRAEL'S</u> school Master <u>until</u> Christ came. If he is really good, he will tell you that Physical Circumcision will not profit you at all in your right standing with God. <u>HE WILL PROCLAIM THAT NO ONE WILL BE JUSTIFIED BY THE LAW IN CHRIST</u>! How many of the statements have you heard?

Then, why on Saturday night will he sneak out like a thief to the Law Library and check out one book ... Malachi Chapter 3? Why would he use this Natural Law on you every Sunday morning? Tithing is Circumcision of the Wallet! There are major contradictions in your pastor's theology! Something is seriously wrong! I will tell you what it is.

God's Law Library Under the New Covenant Has Been Boarded up and Closed Since Calvary!

When Adam and Eve sinned in the Garden of Eden God put an Angel with a flaming sword blocking the way to the tree of life. He did not want mankind to remain in a fallen spiritual state. The Holy Spirit stands on the steps of the Law Library proclaiming that under the New Covenant the Law Library has been closed since Calvary! He Proclaims That No One Will Be Justified by the Law in Christ! The Holy Spirit is the Chief Librarian! The Spirit of Truth has placed a lock on the Law Library door. <u>Those who walk in the Spirit of Truth will not break the lock of truth and enter the Law Library.</u>

He Tells Me That He Has Met Your Pastor Outside on the steps of the Law Library. Instead of Embracing His Conviction They Choose to Walk in Contradiction! The Thief Is Caught!

Like a thief in the night, with the full knowledge of the Grace of God, <u>YOUR</u> <u>PASTOR</u> breaks into the Levitical Law Library. He breaks the Chain of Truth on the door and enters, denying the Voice of Truth's Conviction. He steals <u>ONE</u> <u>LAW</u> all for his benefit! Every Saturday he makes a conscious decision to continue to perpetrate his illusion on you.

A Thief Always Makes a Conscious Decision to Rob You!

Your pastor intentionally refuses to walk by faith and lead by example. Ask yourself how can they study so much and miss the Simple Truths that we have found in our study? Jesus said, "And when He the Spirit of Truth has come, He will guide you into All Truth." Has the Holy Spirit failed in His ability to convict their hearts? Has He failed to guide them into all truth? Nay! Like a horse that is led to the water, they refuse to drink from the Truth of Living Waters found in Christ!

Shame on them!

Malachi Chapter 3: 8
Verse 8 "Will a man rob God?"
Yet you have robbed me!
But you say,
' In what way have we robbed you?
In tithes and offerings.

Let's briefly review the four spiritual principles that we have found in all of scripture in our study on tithing in the Old Testament.

The First Principle We Found in Our Study on Tithing. The tithe was to be eaten by the tither in the presence of God. Free will offerings were exactly that - a free will offering. You did not have to offer a free will offering. Tithes were never collected in the form of money.

The Second Principle We Have Found in Our Study on Tithing. Tithing was to be practiced only on the increase. In all of scripture no one was ever commanded to tithe on a decreasing scale.

The Third Principle We Have Found in Our Study on Tithing. Tithing was an intimate act directly between the tither and God. There was no middleman. The Levite had no portion or inheritance with the tither. God trusted the tither with the tithe.

The Fourth Principle We Have Found in Our Study on Tithing. Give to those in need around you: the widow, the fatherless, and the stranger. This act of kindness glorified God. It was a visible demonstration to those in need that you had the one true God.

With these four principles in mind, it would appear that Malachi's prophecy on robbing God must contain some kind of error. The preponderance of evidence thus far in God's Tithing Principles does not seem to fit into Malachi's dissertation. It not only fits; it will fit perfectly. Wait until You See Who He Was Really Speaking to! When you see that if this does not make your blood boil, then perhaps you are already dead and twice plucked up in your Vain RELIGIOUS Tradition.

I want to ask you some serious questions about tithing. These are questions that are based on a proper interpretation of the law from our study. The simplicity and truth contained within these questions will destroy the one law that YOUR Pastor STEALS from the Law Library every week! Just answer them honestly and realistically. I want to point out the difference between the Physical Interpretation that your pastor delivers to you and the True Spiritual Reality found in scripture. Anyone can observe things after the natural substance of them. For once in your life look past the natural!

We know that God is a spirit. The book of Revelations declares that there are seven spirits of God. The Bible also declares that no man has ever seen God. Let's begin with some real serious common sense questions. Are you ready? I beg you with my whole heart to really stop, think, and consider every question seriously. Within them you will find the Voice of Truth and Genuine Spiritual Reality.

Since We Know That God Is A Spirit, How Could Anyone Be Charged With Robbing Him Of Natural Substances? The Question Is Not "Will a Man Rob God?" But Can You?

Stay focused with me. Your pastor INVOKES the Physical Manifestation of an Old Testament Law every time he collects tithes. He even intentionally interprets it wrong. He will quote, "Will a Man Rob God?" to you with the implication being that this robbery could possibly be a physical reality in your life. I declare, it is not a physical reality at all. It Is Not Even a Physical Possibility! Go ahead, let me see you do it. Since it is physically impossible for you to Rob God of a natural substance, then perhaps God is not speaking about natural things in these passages of scripture. The natural eye will only see the natural and feed the soul its natural desires. Open your spiritual eyes! TO IMPLY THAT THE CREATOR OF ALL THINGS NEEDS YOUR TITHES "IN THE FORM OF MONEY" TO KEEP HIS STOREFRONT OPEN ON THE EARTH IS INTENTIONAL IGNORANT HERESY. Explain to me how the creator that made you from the dust of the earth and breathed life into you would need your help? What can you give God that he has not already given you?

Think Spiritually...Not Physically!

In our study, we found that the tither ate the tithe in the presence of God. HOW THEN COULD YOU, AS THE TITHER, BE CHARGED WITH ROBBING GOD OF SOMETHING THAT HE PROVIDED FOR YOU TO EAT? That one question alone has the power to deliver you from another tithing sermon filled with manipulation, guilt, and condemnation after the law. Since you were to eat the tithe that God provided, how then could you Rob Him? What was really being robbed from God? No where in scripture will you find that tithing was about money. God does not need your money where He is and He cannot spend it. Your money is of no value to God, along with your fleshly faithless acts of tithing!

An Emasculated Cheerleader's Worst Nightmare
Is A Christian with a Brain.
Become ONE!

Keep thinking spiritual! <u>Under the law we found that free will offerings were exactly that. Your Own Free Will!</u> It meant that you could participate in a free will offering or you could not. The choice was yours. <u>Free will offerings were never done by command or compulsion even under the law</u>.

Think Spiritual!

According to Malachi Chapter 3: 8
In what way have we robbed you?
In tithes and offerings.

Since **All** offerings were an act of the free will, how then could **YOU** as a tither be charged with robbing God of something you did not have to do?

How could you as a tither ever be charged with not offering God a free will offering? The entire matter is not about Physical Substance! How many times have you heard, "You Have Robbed Me in My Tithes and Offerings!" The next time you hear that stand up and look the heretic and the thief in the eyes. <u>Confront the one that stands before you in Contradiction and refuses to live by Conviction of the Holy Spirit.</u>

Ask him

How you could Rob God of something that God provided and you were to eat?

Ask him how you can Rob God of a free will offering that was to be an act of your own free will anyhow?

Then, stand back and watch his eyes. They are the mirrors of the soul. In his eyes you will see this expression, "Houston, we have a problem!" Privately he will double-talk you. If he speaks publicly, confront him publicly. Many will answer you arrogantly, "If you don't like it here then leave." Many will try to make you appear less knowledgeable than themselves. __Believe me, they will double talk this book to death.__ Well you see, here ... or there ... is where this guy missed it. Don't buy it! Who knows? You may be instrumental in delivering your pastor from breaking and entering into the Law Library next Saturday night! Do not be afraid of finding a genuine reality in Christ for yourself. You will certainly be able to stop him from perverting your faith, as well as, stop his intentional physical theft by entering your wallet illegally. **He is no better than a pickpocket.** Make no mistake about it; those who practice such things will not inherit the Kingdom of God! For outside of the gates are all ... LIARS AND THIEVES!

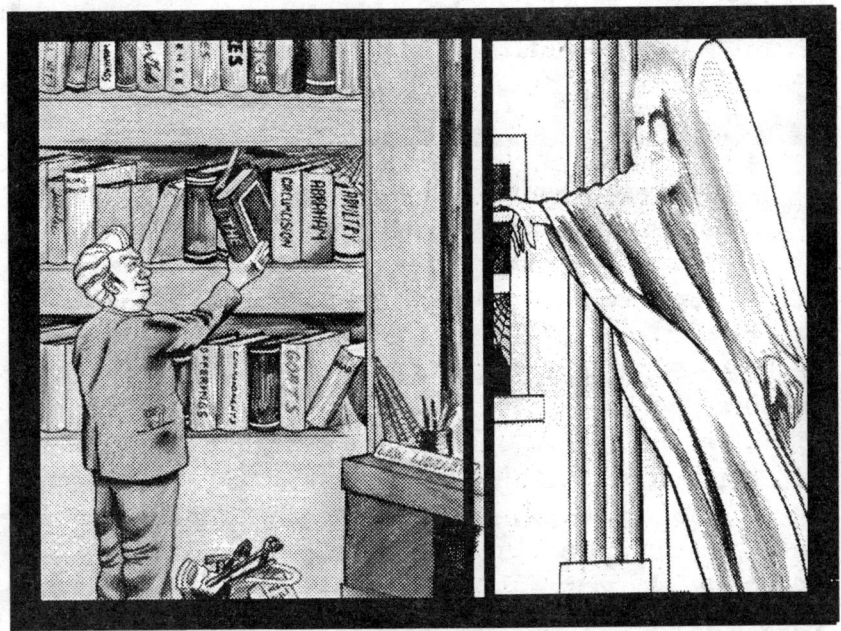

WOE TO THE MAN THAT CONTINUES TO ROB THE CHILDREN OF GOD!

It Gets Even Better!
Mal 3:9-10

> 9   You are cursed with a curse, for you have robbed Me, even this whole nation.
>
> 10   Bring all the tithes into the storehouse, that there may be **food** in My house, and try Me now in this," says the LORD of hosts, "If I will not open for you the windows of heaven and pour out for you such blessing that there will not be room enough to receive it.

Read This Paragraph Two Times

Turn your attention with me to one word in verse ten for now. That word would be the word "FOOD." In the original King James Version of the Bible the word is translated meat. When researched the word meat means food or provision. We have already established that God is a spirit. Since we know that GOD IS NOT A MEAT EATER then who is going to eat this meat? What was the meat for? What was God talking about? Think spiritual! The tither ate the tithe and he did not have to give a free will offering. Certainly, God is not the meat eater! Who was going to eat the meat? Since the tither ate the Tithe, and did not have to offer a free will offering, who then was being charged with Robbing God? What was being Robbed from God? What would invoke such anger from a Holy God that he would tell them, "You are cursed with a curse."

The Answer Must Be Found

Within Our Four Spiritual Principles On Tithing.

The First Principle We Found in Our Study on Tithing. <u>The tithe was eaten by the tither in the presence of God.</u> Free will offerings were exactly that - a free will offering. You did not have to offer a free will offering. Tithes were <u>NEVER</u> collected in the form of money.

The Second Principle Tithing was to be only on the increase. In all of scripture no one was ever commanded to tithe on a decreasing scale.

The Third Principle Tithing was an intimate act <u>directly</u> between the tither and God. There was no middleman. The Levite had no portion or inheritance with the tither. God trusted the tither with the tithe.

The Fourth Principle Give to those in need around you: the widow, fatherless, and the stranger. This act of kindness glorified God. It was a visible demonstration to those in need that you had the one true God.

Our first principle proves that Malachi Chapter 3: 8 is not speaking about natural substance. Our second principle does not apply to these passages because we found that tithing was only on the increase. Our third principle also does not apply because it speaks of the intimate relationship between the tither (you) and God.

It is in our Fourth Principle that we will find the answer to what was being Robbed from God.

Glory!

The Father was being Robbed Of the Glory due Him.

That Glory was to be received by Him, as His Children out of an Intimate Relationship with Him blessed those in need within their community. As this Visible Demonstration of His Sovereign Provision touched the lives of the widows, strangers, and orphans God received glory unto Himself.

"Surely, you have the one true God!"

Saints

You Cannot Rob God of Natural Substance, But You Can Rob Him of the Glory That Is Due Him From Being Expressed Through Your Life!

When you tithe money into the offering plate of a thief that uses the law of tithing, <u>You</u> <u>Are</u> <u>Robbed</u> of an intimate relationship with your Father. <u>The</u> <u>Father</u> <u>is</u> <u>Robbed</u> of the Glory due Him. When you put money in a basket, you throw away Your Responsibility of Hearing God by Faith. <u>YOU</u> <u>DENY</u> your Father the intimacy that He desires with you. <u>YOU</u> deny Him the right to express Himself through you in genuine love.

Quit religious tradition and grow into Spiritual Reality and Intimacy with the Father. The lives that you can touch while you are here are what are important to God. When the role is called up yonder it will not be about your money. It will be about Faith, Intimacy, and the Sovereign Glory of God being expressed through <u>YOUR LIFE.</u> Is that happening? You must stop denying the Father His Sovereign right to touch the lives of those around you that are in need.

The reason God wanted "THE FOOD" was because He was going to take care of the strangers, widows, and orphans. The Father was being Robbed of the Glory due Him. He was also being Robbed of the Intimacy and Fellowship with His children. There is no other logical reason why God wanted food or provision in his house. "That there may be meat in my house." God <u>COULD NOT CHARGE THE TITHER</u> with fault because he was to EAT his tithe. God <u>COULD NOT CHARGE THE TITHER</u> with failure to bring a free will offering that the tither did not have to bring.

We now know that it was The Glory that was being Robbed from God. WHO THEN WAS THE THIEF? <u>WHO WAS RESPONSIBLE FOR THE THEFT OF THE GLORY OF GOD? WHO WAS KEEPING THE CHILDREN OF GOD FROM FELLOWSHIP AND INTIMACY WITH THE FATHER?</u>

It Is Time for Your Blood to Boil!

A Corrupt Priesthood
Stealing Meat
**In the Old Testament
Is Not any different
Than A Pastor That
"Uses" The Law
To Collect Money
And Build A Church.
Both are Evil!**

The Latter Is An "Illusion of Reality!"

It Was the Levitical Priesthood That Was Robbing God Not You ... or the Tither!

All of Malachi 3:8-10
Is Directed and Spoken to the Priesthood!
It Was An Open Rebuke Of Their Evil Practices!

Without a doubt we have proven that tithing was not about money. We have proven that nothing physical **can** or was being robbed from God. Undeniably, the only thing that was being robbed from God in Malachi Chapter 3: 8 was the Glory Due His Holy Name.

That Glory Was Being Stopped From Flowing Through The Lives Of God's Children Because The **Priests In The Temple Were Corrupt!**

The Pastoral Thief that breaks into the Law Library and intentionally preaches this Malachi junk to you is every bit as corrupt, if not MORE. He knows that it was the Levitical Priesthood that was corrupt. He intentionally fails to point out to you the scriptures that we are about to look at.

I urge you to fill your heart with this understanding. **Please, take the time to read the scriptures.** I went through the additional expense of printing all of the scriptures in this book to insure that you would gain understanding. Please read them.

A Brief Study In History

Israel from the moment God delivered them from Egypt had a problem serving God by faith. The book is filled with their wandering ways. (Not unlike many believers today.) Many times God drove them into exile because of their faithless behavior. There were good Kings and bad Kings. The priesthood historically was corrupt on numerous occasions.

THE PRIESTS IN THE OLD TESTAMENT ROBBED THE PEOPLE MANY TIMES. THIS INCIDENT IN MALACHI IS NOT ANY DIFFERENT.

The climax of that corruption was evident when Jesus appeared in the New Testament. The Levitical priesthood in Jesus' day was historically one of the most corrupt. Their corruption and reliance upon the law and its power was what drove them to Crucify Christ. He was a threat to the established order of religion in that day.

Before we look at the Corruption of the Priesthood in Malachi, I would like to point out another example. This corruption was such a blatant, horrendous evil that it would cause God to kill the priest and his sons. May your eyes be opened.

1 Sam 2:12-17

12 Now the sons of Eli were corrupt; they did not know the LORD.

13 And the priests' custom with the people was that when any man offered a sacrifice, the priest's servant would come with a three-pronged fleshhook in his hand while the meat was boiling.

14 Then he would thrust it into the pan, or kettle, or caldron, or pot; and the priest would take for himself all that the fleshhook brought up. So they did in Shiloh to all the Israelites who came there.

15 Also, before they burned the fat, the priest's servant would come and say to the man who sacrificed, "Give meat for roasting to the priest, for he will not take boiled meat from you, but raw."

16 And if the man said to him, "They should really burn the fat first; then you may take as much as your heart desires," he would then answer him, "No, but you must give it now; and if not, I will take it by force."

17 Therefore the sin of the young men was very great before the LORD, for men abhorred the offering of the LORD.

(NKJ)

In this incident it is clear that Eli's sons were Robbing the Children of God. They were also Robbing God! They were not only stealing the meat; they evidently were reselling it. They did not want the meat boiled because they could not resell it.

<u>This Evil Priesthood Caused The Tither To Abhor The Offering Of The Lord.</u> The People Would Eventually Stop Coming, **Like Many That Are <u>Wise</u> and Remain Outside of The Church Today!**

We will see that the evil priesthood in Malachi Chapters
1 through 3 were not much different.

1 Sam 2:22-25

Read

22   Now Eli was very old; and he heard everything
his sons did to all Israel, and **how** **they** **lay** **with**
the **women** **who** **assembled** **at** **the** **door** **of**
the **tabernacle** **of** **meeting.**
23   So he said to them, "Why do you do such things?
For I hear of your evil dealings from all the people.
24   "No, my sons! For it is not a good report that I
hear. **You** **make** **the** **LORD'S** **people**
transgress.
25   "If one man sins against another, God will judge
him. But if a man sins against the LORD, who will
intercede for him?" Nevertheless, they did not heed the
voice of their father, because the LORD desired to kill
them.(NKJ)

The Evil Sons of Eli
Were the Reason
The People Transgressed.
We Will Find THIS Same Reason
In the Priesthood in
Malachi!

1 Sam 2:27-34
Read, We Are Going Somewhere
I Promise You!

27   Then a man of God came to Eli and said to him, "Thus says the LORD: 'Did I not clearly reveal Myself to the house of your father when they were in Egypt in Pharaoh's house?

28   'Did I not choose him out of all the tribes of Israel to be My priest, to offer upon My altar, to burn incense, and to wear an ephod before Me? And did I not give to the house of your father all the offerings of the children of Israel made by fire?

29   <u>'Why do you kick at My sacrifice and My offering which I have commanded in My dwelling place, and honor your sons more than Me, to make yourselves fat with the best of all the offerings of Israel My people?'</u>

30   "Therefore the LORD God of Israel says: 'I said indeed that your house and the house of your father would walk before Me forever.' But now the LORD says: 'Far be it from Me; for those who honor Me I will honor, and those who despise Me shall be lightly esteemed.

31   'Behold, the days are coming that I will cut off your arm and the arm of your father's house, so that there will not be an old man in your house.

32   'And you will see an enemy in My dwelling place, despite all the good which God does for Israel. And there shall not be an old man in your house forever.

33   'But any of your men whom I do not cut off from My altar shall consume your eyes and grieve your heart. And all the descendants of your house shall die in the flower of their age.

34   <u>'Now this shall be a sign to you that will come upon your two sons, on Hophni and Phinehas: in one day they shall die, both of them.</u>

35   <u>And I will raise me up a faithful priest, that shall do according to that which is in mine heart and in my mind: and I will build him a sure house; and he shall walk before mine anointed for ever.(NKJ)</u>

Once again, I urge you to listen to the language in the manner in which God speaks to Eli. Most of these passages could be copied and pasted directly into the book of Malachi. If you will really read these scriptures you will not believe the stark resemblance that we will find in Malachi.

Here is a question to think about: Would God Charge The Tither with Error When **His** Priesthood Was Corrupt and Evil?

God is not Unfair Or Hypocritical.

1 Sam 4:15-18

15   Eli was ninety-eight years old, and his eyes were so dim that he could not see.

16   Then the man said to Eli, "I am he who came from the battle. And I fled today from the battle line." And he said, "What happened, my son?"

17   So the messenger answered and said, "Israel has fled before the Philistines, and there has been a great slaughter among the people. Also your two sons, Hophni and Phinehas, are dead; and the ark of God has been captured."

18   Then it happened, when he made mention of the ark of God, that Eli fell off the seat backward by the side of the gate; and his neck was broken and he died, for the man was old and heavy. And he had judged Israel forty years. (NKJ)

Come Lord and Purge Your House
Of the Eli's In This Generation.
Begin With Paul Cain,
A False Prophet.
The Eli ... Of Our Day!

This example of Eli and his sons are typical of how corrupt the priesthood had become on many occasions. When the book of Malachi was written the priesthood was equally corrupt. It was, in my opinion, more corrupt than Eli and his evil sons. The Levitical priesthood reached the pinnacle of its corruption by the time Jesus arrived. Today I believe it is at the same pinnacle. "No, my sons!" For it is not a good report that I hear. You make the LORD'S people transgress. Eli understood that the Corrupt actions of the priesthood were what caused the people to transgress.

MALACHI'S ENTIRE PROPHECY IS DIRECTED AT THE PRIESTHOOD. The tither bears little responsibility for Robbing God. The tither can only be charged with failure to obediently continue to do what he was told even with a corrupt priesthood. He was to come and have a Meal with The Father. That Meal was being stolen By The Corrupt Priesthood.

No matter where you go to Church I assure you according to ALL Scripture Your Meal With The Father is being Stolen From You by "The Lie of The Tithe."

This Is Extremely Important!

With scripture from the book of Malachi, we will see that God was very angry with the Levitical priesthood. They were responsible for the statement, "Will a Man Rob God?" They were also responsible for, " You Are Cursed with a Curse." GOD WAS REBUKING THE LEVITICAL PRIESTHOOD, NOT THE TITHER. If you are tired at this point, I ask you to put this book down and take a break. This is as important for you to understand as it was to understand that the tither ate the tithe.

When you read scripture always remember to keep it in its proper context of who is speaking to whom. Never pick it up and immediately apply it to you.

None of Malachi's Rebuke
Of the Levitical priesthood Applies to You!

Malachi Chapter 1

1   The burden of the word of the LORD to Israel by Malachi. (NKJ)

The word spoken was to Israel. It was not spoken to you. You cannot equate God speaking to Moses, Noah, or even Pharaoh as being something that would apply directly to you. While there is an abundance of truth contained within scripture, you must be careful not to pull things out of context. It is theological suicide for anyone to try and make everything fit to you personally. We need a fresh understanding of the Grace of God. This book is about that Grace. The word delivered by Malachi was to a corrupt and evil Levitical priesthood. Not to You!

Mal 1:6-10
A Corrupt Priesthood
Read ... Especially the Underlined Parts

6   "A son honors his father, and a servant his master. If then I am the Father, where is My honor? And if I am a Master, where is My reverence? Says the LORD of hosts to you priests who despise My name. Yet you say, 'In what way have we despised Your name?'

7   "You offer defiled food on My altar. But say, 'In what way have we defiled You?' By saying, 'The table of the LORD is contemptible.'

8   And when you offer the blind as a sacrifice, is it not evil? And when you offer the lame and sick, is it not evil? Offer it then to your governor! Would he be pleased with you? Would he accept you favorably?" Says the LORD of hosts.

9   "But now entreat God's favor, that He may be gracious to us. While this is being done by your hands, will He accept you favorably?" Says the LORD of hosts.

10   "Who is there even among you who would shut the doors, so that you would not kindle fire on My altar in vain? I have no pleasure in you," says the LORD of hosts, "Nor will I accept an offering from your hands. (NKJ)

In the very first Chapter God charges the Levitical priesthood with offering blind, lame, sick, and defiled food on His altar. He charges them with being evil. He tells them "I have no pleasure in you!" He closes by saying, "Nor will I accept an offering from your hands." Whose hands? The Levitical priesthood's hands! In verse nine God offered them a chance to repent. Even "while this is being done by your hands." We will find this offer again in Chapter 3.

It should be obvious to you that the Levitical priesthood was extremely corrupt and that God was speaking to them. Make a mental note of the questions asked by these priests.

'In what way Have WE despised Your name?'
'In what way have We defiled You?'

Those two questions are in the same context and tone that we will find in the question in Chapter 3 ...

' IN WHAT WAY HAVE WE ROBBED YOU?

God was not speaking to the tither in that day or to you in this day! The Levitical priesthood at this point had to be stealing the good stuff for themselves just like Eli's evil sons. I would have to say the priesthood of Malachi had to be worse. They were in total substitution keeping the good meat for themselves, while offering the sick, blind, and the lame to God. It is evident that they had fallen completely away from God. There was no fear within them for such evil behavior. I would encourage you to read all of Chapter 1 in Malachi.

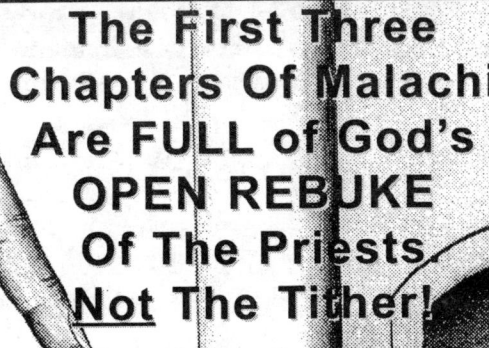

The First Three
Chapters Of Malachi
Are FULL of God's
OPEN REBUKE
Of The Priests,
Not The Tither!

Mal 2:1-9 It Gets Worse!

Read ... Double Read the Underlined Parts!

1   "And now, <u>O priests, this commandment IS FOR YOU</u>.

2   <u>IF YOU</u> will not hear, and if you will not take it to heart, <u>to give glory to My name</u>," says the LORD of hosts, "<u>I will send a curse upon you, and I will curse your blessings. Yes, I have cursed them already, because you do not take it to heart.</u>

3   "Behold, I will rebuke your descendants and spread refuse on your faces, the refuse of your solemn feasts; and one will take you away with it.

4   Then you shall know that I have sent this commandment to you, that My covenant with Levi may continue," says the LORD of hosts.

5   "My covenant was with him, one of life and peace, and I gave them to him that he might fear Me; so he feared Me and was reverent before My name.

6   The law of truth was in his mouth, and injustice was not found on his lips. He walked with Me in peace and equity, and turned many away from iniquity.

7   "<u>For the lips of a priest should keep knowledge, and people should seek the law from his mouth; for he is the messenger of the LORD of hosts.</u>

8   <u>But you have departed from the way; you have caused many to stumble at the law. You have corrupted the covenant of Levi,</u>" says the LORD of hosts.

9   "<u>Therefore I also have made you contemptible and base before all the people, because you have not kept My ways but have shown partiality in the law.</u>" (NKJ)

In Chapter 1 we found that God was chastising the Levitical priesthood. In Chapter 2 He does not let up. This command is for YOU ... <u>0 Priests!</u>
<u>He tells them again that they are "Cursed with a curse."</u>

God makes it very Clear
That their Actions
Failed
To give Him
The Glory Due
His Name.

An important observation for you to understand is that His curse in verse two was upon their blessings. Remember this and that context when you read about God opening the Windows of heaven and pouring out a blessing in Chapter 3. God was so angry that He promised to smear some pretty dirty stuff on the faces of their descendants. These passages are nearly identical in content with the passages of scripture we examined about Eli and his evil sons.

Vs. 4 through 7 explains what a priesthood was supposed to be like. The Father gives a clear picture to the corrupt priesthood in Malachi of how far they had fallen from the integrity and honor of Levi.

In Verse Eight He Tells the Corrupt Priests
<u>That</u> <u>They</u> <u>Alone</u>
<u>Have</u> <u>Caused</u> <u>Many</u> <u>to</u> <u>Stumble</u>.

Would a Just God Charge the People with Error
When <u>HIS</u> Priesthood Was Evil and Corrupt?

In verse nine God continues to chastise them by telling them that He has made them <u>contemptible</u> <u>in</u> <u>the</u> <u>eyes</u> <u>of</u> <u>the</u> <u>people.</u> This was a slap at their posture of arrogance. About this time you should realize that there is absolutely no way that Malachi Chapter 3 would/could apply to the Tither. God had <u>CHARGED</u> <u>THE</u> <u>PRIESTHOOD</u> <u>WITH</u> <u>CAUSING</u> <u>MANY</u> <u>TO</u> <u>STUMBLE.</u> He had made the priesthood to appear in the eyes of the people as contemptible as a nazi to a Jew. At this point, to even assume that you have any obligation under Malachi Chapter 3 to pay tithes is ludicrous. I hope that the thief we caught in the Law Library is beginning to appear to you as contemptible as this corrupt Levitical priesthood was. Your pastor intentionally perverts the truth! It is really quite simple; just keep track of to whom is God Speaking. <u>You</u> <u>Talk'n</u> <u>To</u> <u>ME?</u>

No! You Talk'n To **THEM.**

God Continues to Speak to The Corrupt Priesthood!
From Malachi Chapter 1 to the beginning of Chapter 3 God is STILL speaking
To the PRIESTS ... <u>NOT</u> The Tither

Mal 3:1-7
Verse 1 and 2
Are Prophetic about the coming priesthood of Christ

1   "Behold, I send My messenger, and he will prepare the way before Me. And the Lord, whom you seek, will suddenly come to His temple, even the Messenger of the covenant, in whom you delight. Behold, He is coming," says the LORD of hosts.

2   "But who can endure the day of His coming? And who can stand when He appears? For He is like a refiner's fire and like launderer's soap.

3   He will sit as a refiner and a purifier of silver; <u>he will purify the sons of Levi,</u> and purge them as gold and silver, that they may offer to the LORD an offering in righteousness.

4   "Then the offering of Judah and Jerusalem will be pleasant to the LORD, as in the days of old, as in former years.

5   <u>And I will come near YOU for judgment; I will be a swift witness against sorcerers, against adulterers, against perjurers, against those who exploit wage earners and widows and orphans, and against those who turn away an alien— because they do not fear Me," says the LORD of hosts.</u>

6   "For I am the LORD, I do not change; therefore you are not consumed, O sons of Jacob.

7   Yet from the days of your fathers <u>you have gone away from My ordinances and have not kept them.</u> Return to Me, and I will return to you," says the LORD of hosts. "<u>But you said, 'In what way shall we return?'</u>(NKJ)

" **Purify the Sons of Levi**" continues to demonstrate that God was still speaking to the Levitical priesthood in Israel in that day. Not to you, or your day! I do feel that we could sure use some purifying among the Levites of our day. The prophetic word about the coming priesthood of Christ mirrors how corruptible the priesthood had been throughout history. In Chapter 1 God was speaking to the Levites. In Chapter 2 we found the same thing. It should be no surprise to you that God is also speaking directly to the Levites in Chapter 3. If this does not make your blood boil, I do not know what will. The number of times that you have been intentionally deceived with these scriptures is as wicked as the Levitical priesthood!

Here Is the Heart of the Matter!

It is found in Verse Five.

"Against Those Who Exploit Wage Earners
And Widows and Orphans, and against Those
Who Turn Away an Alien—"

This is the very heart of God. All of His anger was against this corrupt priesthood. Because of their corrupt evil behavior, the Levitical priesthood had caused many to "stumble at the law." The tither had become totally disillusioned with the priesthood.

God said that the priesthood would be "contemptible" in the eyes of the people. The result of a corrupt priesthood always caused the tither to stumble at the law. It also immediately Robbed God of the Glory due Him. Every evil priesthood immediately perverted the visible reality of God's kindness from being demonstrated through the lives of His children. That Glory was expressed through His children to the widows, orphans, and the strangers within the land.

That Glory was what Was being Robbed from God. It was NOT about Money!

I do not believe the filthy, sick, blind, and lame sacrifices that were being offered by the Levites angered God as much as this Theft of His Glory. The Evil Levitical Priesthood in Malachi was responsible for desecrating the Image and Glory of God to the nations. God is just as angry with the thieves who desecrate the Blood of Christ with Contradiction. Woe to the man that knowingly uses the law to extract money from the children of God! There is your thief and robber of God!

When we look at Verse 7 there is only one conclusion possible. God was speaking to the Levites! " Yet from the days of your fathers you have gone away from My ordinances and have not kept them. Return to Me, and I will return to you." God was speaking to the Levites from the beginning of this Chapter, as well as, throughout the Entire Book of Malachi.

Here Comes That Question
That I Asked You to Make a Mental Note About.
"But you said, 'In what way shall we return?'

"But YOU said! Who said? The Levitical Priesthood said, 'In what way shall we return?' Just like they had said in Chapter 1: 6 'In what way have WE despised Your name?' They also proclaimed in Chapter 1: 7 'In what way have WE defiled You?'

Is It Any Wonder to You Why God Would Tell **Them** **You** Have Robbed Me!

This should be obvious to you by now. I would encourage you to read the first three Chapters of Malachi completely. Take a sheet of paper and keep track of to whom God is speaking. I took this extra time to point out to you the undeniable truth that God was angry with the priesthood. The Tither is not mentioned or charged with error by God anywhere in Malachi. God had made the priesthood look "contemptible" in the eyes of the Tither. Our four spiritual principles on tithing will destroy every sermon you have ever heard about tithing from Malachi Chapter 3, "Will a Man Rob God?"

You really do not need another example from the Spirit of Truth to be free from the bondage of the law. I do not know anyone that has ever sat on a pew and not felt the sting and guilt inflicted from the phrase, "Will a Man Rob God?" You cannot sit on a pew with a heart of love for God and not feel the manipulation and condemnation by the speaker. THAT IS, UNLESS YOU ARE JUST A RELIGIOUS GOAT JUST PRACTICING RELIGION WITHOUT REALLY KNOWING GOD.

The Kingdom of God Is Within You! Going to Church does not prove that you know God. A building is not the House of God. YOU ARE!

Isn't it ironic how the speaker within the Tithe Collecting Religious Institutions will try each week to impart an understanding of HOW YOU SHOULD LIVE A LIFE OF FAITH? Yet, they fail to allow faith to establish them. They intentionally use The Law of Tithing every week in order to keep their doors open. Don't tell me that they do "Good Works." Many Non-Christian organizations far exceed the "good works" done by your little Holy Huddle you call a Church!

Like a Thief
They intentionally
Need the Law Library
In order to keep
Their Man Made
Illusion Alive.
However, in your hard time,
you my friend, will have to
learn to live by faith.
Contradiction is Hypocrisy.
What Hypocrites They Are!

Some of you have been Tithing so long that you cannot begin to comprehend how a Church could exist without Tithe Money.

You Must Not Fear the Loss Of Man's Illusion To find Deeper Reality of God

Wait until you see what we will find in the New Testament. <u>There was a Church that was a Living Breathing Reality Of Christ. IT DID NOT Collect Tithes!</u> WHAT DO YOU SIT IN?

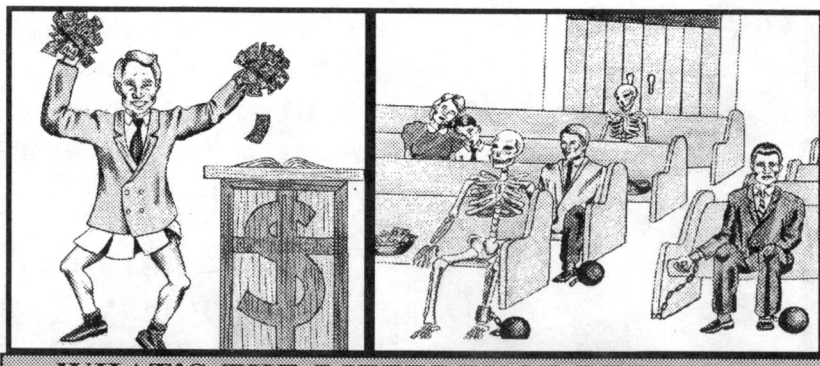

WHAT'S THE DIFFERENCE BETWEEN AN USHER AND A VULTURE?
FEATHERS!

It Is Time to Purge
The Levites of Our Day!
To Catch a Thief?

We Did!

In the Law Library!
Remember, It Is Not
"Will a Man Rob God?"
But Can He?

Be Free!

Come to reality, intimacy, and fellowship with your Father. Allow Him to build in and through your life what He desires. Allow Him to express His loving kindness to those around you in need. Give Him The Glory Due Him From Your Life!

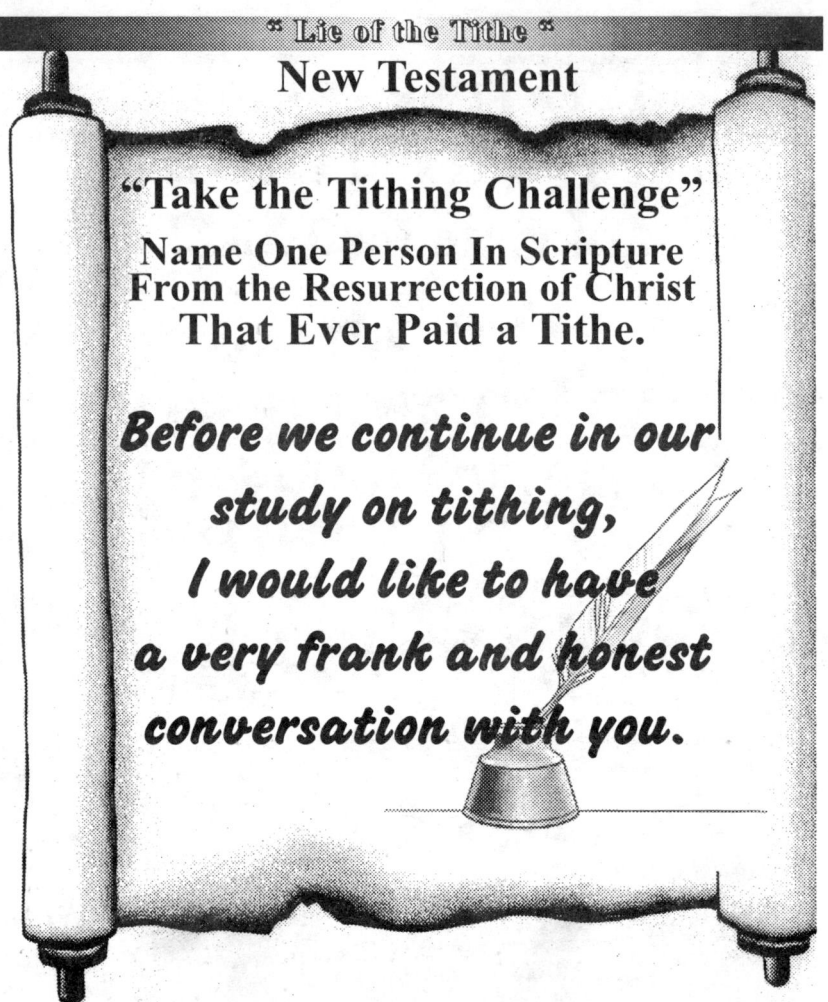

New Testament

"Take the Tithing Challenge"

Name One Person In Scripture From the Resurrection of Christ That Ever Paid a Tithe.

Before we continue in our study on tithing, I would like to have a very frank and honest conversation with you.

I want to speak to you about Reality, the Tangible Visible Reality of God in your life. Please do not quickly answer, "I know God." You are probably right; you may know Him to some degree. God may have revealed Himself to you somewhere along life's way. However, that does not mean that you have an Intimate, Tangible Reality of God in your life. While this book addresses the illegal collection of money from the children of God, it actually has several purposes. It also addresses the reality of genuine biblical faith in your life.

This book will also expose the theft of your intimacy and faith with God. The entire intent of this book is to challenge your faith in order to draw you into a Deeper Reality of God in your life.

My manner of speaking is to provoke you to think about what you believe. It is time for you to sit and seriously think about how you came to believe what you believe. If you will be honest with yourself <u>most of what you believe is based on what the pulpit has told you.</u> While I am very outspoken about the charlatans of our day and the pulpits intentional deception,

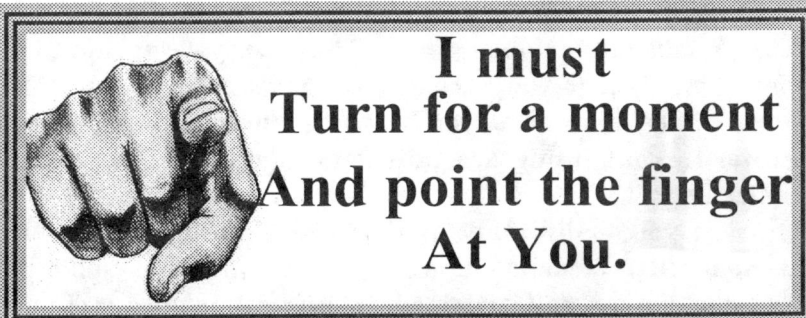

I must
Turn for a moment
And point the finger
At You.

You are also responsible for practicing religion instead of finding a true reality of God in your life. You were supposed to read the book and search a matter out for yourself. Anytime you accept the word of anyone without searching the matter out for yourself, you have no one to blame but yourself.

You will never stand before God with this argument, "That's what he told me to do." "I just did what they said." You alone have the divine responsibility and privilege of really knowing God for yourself. Jesus tore down the religious establishment of His day. He warned the people to, "Beware of the leaven of the Pharisees!" This was a warning that the doctrine and practices of the Pharisees were extremely dangerous to their soul. Exposing the serious destruction of a life by the legalistic religious system was a <u>Very Large Part</u> of Jesus' ministry. Jesus told the Pharisees at one point that everyone they converted into their religious practice became "Twice the sons of the devil."

Religion
Perverts
The Truth
And Sell$
That Falsehood
As A Reality!

Take the time to Read Matthew Chapter 23 carefully. Jesus hated religion and its destructive power on the soul. Religion is the worst evil known to man. Sin is no longer a problem. Evil still exists and the theft of your soul is found on a Religious Pew. Religion perverts the truth and Sells that Falsehood as a Reality. Everyone that practices religion falls into an open grave. That is why Jesus said to the Pharisees, "Woe to you, scribes and Pharisees, hypocrites! For you are like whitewashed tombs which indeed appear beautiful outwardly, but inside are full of dead men's bones and all uncleanness."

If you really think about it, the Son of God publicly pronounced destruction upon the very religious system that God the Father had ordained. Jesus condemned, rebuked, exposed, and openly confronted the religious leaders of His day. He did this because of the intentionally deceptive doctrines of men that had totally corrupted the Temple into a Legalistic Religious Institution. The Temple and the ordinances ordained by God had become destructive to the eternal souls of the people. It was full of the dead men's bones (the people who came) and all uncleanness. God was not within a thousand miles of it. That religious system that Jesus denounced and exposed is still absent from the earth to this day. Prophetically this proves that Jesus was every bit of who He said He was. Only one person would have the power and authority to destroy the Temple and its functions.

The Temple in Jerusalem is gone forever. However, religion and its death is still alive and well on the planet. If you will study the corruption of the Temple and the Priesthood, you will begin to understand why Jesus was so adamant about exposing its Religious Corruption. He left us with a Visible understanding of what God **DOES NOT WANT!**

Only one person would have the Power and Authority to destroy the Temple in Jerusalem that God Himself had ordained. That would have to be the Son of God Himself. "All Power and Authority has been given to the Son." Simply put, Jesus passed judgment on two things during His life and ministry. Jesus accepted full payment and judgment for sin upon Himself. Secondly, Jesus Judged and Exposed Man's Religious System. He pronounced such severe judgment "not one stone will be left standing." Its total destruction is still evident to this day.

I suppose that if Jesus were to show up today that He would have to take the same position with our Man Made religious system and its Leaders. If He did not, then He would have to apologize for destroying the Pharisees of His day. Within Him you will not find hypocrisy or shadows of turning. Many churches today are polished on the outside of the cup, but on the inside they are full of dead men's bones, (you) and corruption. What is taking place in our day is a thousand times worse than what took place in the Pharisees of Jesus' day.

> **They Practiced the Law to Perfection, We Prostitute Grace to Perfection.**

I am intentionally confrontational to the destructive patterns of religion and the religious traditions of man. This is my calling. I do not apologize for finding God's Purpose for my life. My Father and your Father spoke to me very clearly many years ago about my Purpose in the Kingdom of God. Behold I am sending you to a stiff necked and hard hearted people. Do Not fear them or their looks ... For I have made your forehead harder than theirs! I offer no apologies for the words I use. I will stand alone accountable before my maker, as will you. Shall I apologize to you for the Strength and Power of My Source?

More than you realize I wrestle for your soul against an eternal enemy of God. The subtle theft has been in your relationship with God ... more than your pocketbook.

No one can know God for you, not your Mommy, Daddy, the preacher, your uncle, or anyone. Religion will offer you a false security that will not be redeemable at the end of your life. The grave has received many like yourself for thousands of years. The grave is full of useless corpses, people like you who came here and never found out why they were really here. The laughter heard in the Spirit World every time a life departs that is void of Reality, Intimacy, and Purpose from God echoes throughout the heavenlies. The hardest question you will ever ask yourself is <u>Why You Are Really Here.</u> Was it to raise a family, or perhaps have a great career? Maybe you think it was to get saved and know God. All are useless chaff in the Kingdom Family Business! What is your Function in the Kingdom Family Business? Religion will rob you of your Purpose and Destiny with God. Trust me, I fully understand the death and entrapment found within religious tradition. My Father trained me well for His purpose. I can point you towards the Kingdom Purpose of God your Father, but you must take the steps to Find and Know HIM!

Do You Have Religion Or Reality? Answer These Questions. None of These Practices Are in the Book

Do you practice infant Baptism or baby dedication? Do you have nights of Visitation services? Do you pay Tithes? Are you encouraged to the point of feeling guilty if you miss church service? Do you feel compelled to be in church two or three times a week? Do you attend church more than once a week? Does your church have an altar call at the end of a service? Do you have altar workers? Are you involved in a home cell group that is under the direction of the church?

Does your church ask visitors to stand? Do they have cookies or juice for visitors after the service? Do you pray to Mary? Do you put ashes on your forehead? Do you get together with a group of people and pray in Tongues? Are you involved in a Church Building Program? Does the speaker in your church wear a Robe or Special Religious clothing? Does he wear a Religious Hat? Do you think that your church is the right way? Does your church keep a membership role? Are people invited to become members publicly? Do you feel that your denomination is the best? Are appeals made for people to join your church? Do you attend Sunday School? Does your Church have Ushers? Does your Church pass out a program schedule for the services? Do you have holy water? Is your church service normally a certain length of time? Do you have back-to-back church services? Do you watch a lot of Christian television? I could go on for 500 pages. So How many did you answer yes to? Welcome to the Man Made Religion of this Generation! None of this stuff is in the Book!

Answer the Real questions that pertain to Life. Be honest with yourself. One of the hardest things that I have found to do is to get a Religious Goat to be honest with their own heart.

When Was the Last Time God Spoke Directly to You?
Why Are You Here, What Is Your Purpose In the Kingdom Family Business?

I am not speaking about your job or your home making abilities. How many years do you claim to know God? Then why don't you know why you are here? The church was not to be a place where you sat on a pew (dead men's bones) until you died! The church was not to become a Dead Sea with NO Way Out! It was not to become a building for more and more people to sit.

The Larger the Church, the Bigger the Dead Sea.

You were supposed to find Purpose and then be Released into the Fulfillment of that Purpose. You will never become Fruitful and Fulfilled in Life until you find out why you came to the planet. Why are you really here? Until you find your God given Purpose everything else in your life has been <u>VANITY</u>. The very search for this reality will send you on a deep walk of faith to know God. Only you can pursue this! Without an answer to why you are here the grave awaits you with open arms and laughter.

You will only find out why you are here when you Really become Intimate with your Father. Without your pursuit of that Personal Intimacy, He reveals nothing to you. Begin by walking away from another dime of Religious Tithing. Your Father would never have you contribute to such a foolish death trap. Jesus despised the Evil of Religion and exposed its destructive Power on the soul. What are you doing as a Child of the king enabling and empowering that Evil with your filthy money? The danger of this book is that you will not be able to explain it away. God will tell you that he sent me to warn you of the soon impending judgment upon those who stand and speak saying that they are His when they are not!

When you seriously develop an intimate relationship with God, you will lose a lot of flesh. In the end, you will no longer possess your own life. When that finally happens God will Fill You with HIS Purpose!

The religious establishment of our day is certainly more wicked than it was in Jesus' day. Men today are self-appointed and not anointed. They stand behind the pulpit claiming to be a leader called by God. When in fact, they are nothing more than generic businessmen. When I went to Ministry School I could have Gone to Dallas Theological <u>CEMETERY!</u> The great Baptist Preacher Machine. All you had to do was Graduate and they had a Church waiting for you at a Starting Salary of around $50,000.00. Sounds Like A Business, Smells Like A Business ... IT IS A BUSINESS!

Religion has always been big business. Do you really believe that God needs about 1200 different denominations in this nation alone? If these leaders are from God, then why is the church the most ridiculed institution on the planet? The supposed leaders of our day are not anointed leaders sent by God. Open your eyes, be honest, and Quit Choosing to remain Spiritually Blind.

You alone have the responsibility to enter into a life changing relationship with your Father. It will never come while you are sitting on a pew practicing religion and paying your tithes. God is not within a thousand miles of that system. There is no life in It! Jesus tore it down, " Not one stone will be left standing." You must begin to challenge your heart <u>AND</u> God if you really want to know Him. Like Jacob, do not be afraid to challenge God to prove Himself to you! Just ask Him for a Deeper Spiritual Reality of Christ in your life. He loves to do that. <u>Then Quit Practicing the Law of Tithing, Quit Religious Tradition, and Seek Reality with your Whole Heart.</u> Do you want religion or reality?

> ## YOU DECIDE ... <u>The Grave Awaits You</u>
> ### With Open Arms and Laughter.
> ### It has received many
> ### Dead Men's Bones prior to Yours!

Most People That Attend Church Do So For Various Reasons.

If you are a typical churchgoer, your Sunday religious activities are probably something like this. You wake up on Sunday morning, take a shower, and get dressed for Sunday service. Your service probably begins somewhere between 9 a.m. and 12 noon. When you arrive at church there is a little group of people that know you. Each of you will normally exchange smiles, handshakes, and a few nice words before and after the service. If you have been attending your church for some time, you more than likely have a certain spot or section that you normally sit in. Most of the people that sit around you are rather familiar with you because they sit in their own little spot also. This is your own little circle of church friends, or more appropriately called, your own little "Religious Holy Huddle."

While in church you will have the typical menu of music and sing a few hymns. Perhaps, someone will sing a solo. In most cases, this is normally done when the tithes and offerings are taken. The pulpit will have at least one joke or amusing comment to make you smile. They will reaffirm that it is good for you to be in the house of God today. It is not God's house. You are God's house. Many of you will have a paper program to follow along. This way you will know when to sit, stand, sing, and shut up. Isn't it wonderful to see that God is so boring and systematic? What ever happened to allowing God the divine privilege of orchestrating the service by the Holy Spirit Himself? You will pay your Tithe and possibly feel good about being a part of God's work.

Your Tithe Declares That You Are God's Little Helper On The Earth. You Are Helping Him Reach The Lost And Your Church to DO GOOD ... RIGHT? The sermon may speak to you, bore you, or put you to sleep. So will any motivational speaker in the world. <u>Wait</u> <u>Until</u> <u>You</u> <u>Hear</u> <u>Where</u> <u>These</u> <u>Cheerleaders</u> <u>Get</u> <u>Their</u> <u>Sermons!</u>

Perhaps, there will be a solemn moment at the end of the service for you to reflect briefly. <u>After</u> <u>All</u> <u>God</u> <u>Is</u> <u>There</u> ... Right? On the other hand, the pulpit may give God the opportunity to save another lost soul that could be visiting your little holy huddle. "Oh sinners come home" could be playing softly in the background as the pulpit makes an appeal. Evidently, God has problems operating without mood music.

Depending on your denomination your service will last anywhere from 40 minutes to two hours. The Catholics will normally be the closest denomination to a 40-minute service. <u>QUICK COMMUNION AND OUT THE DOOR!</u> Two hours is reserved for the Charismatic Fanatics. We will leave the Baptists at their typical well-orchestrated one-hour service. You can add 10 minutes for visitors, new membership, and an altar call, complete with mood music.

The restaurant business is well aware that on Sundays the Catholics, Presbyterians, Lutherans, and Episcopals are normally the early crowd. Followed by the Baptists who want to make sure the roast in the oven does not burn. Last to arrive at the restaurant would be the charismatics. After all, <u>in their minds</u> they have been praising the Lord in a greater depth than everyone else.

If you are a typical churchgoer, you will return next week to repeat the Dead Sea process all over again. You will continue to go through the same moronic behavior week after week and year after year. Some of you have been snared by this religious deception for so long that you actually believe this is the way God does business. You think paying Tithes and Religious church attendance is God's purpose for your life. He will reveal to you one day that what you are really doing is conveniently fitting God into your life.

If This is You ... If You are The Typical Church Goer Week After Week ... Year After Year

God is not impressed with your Holy Huddle Church attendance. You have never surrendered to his Sovereign Right to Use You for His purpose. Caught in the traditions of men and the ordinances of religion, you are not really changing. Real change will only come when you find and embrace God's Purpose. You may quit a habit or two, big deal! So have many others who do not claim to know God at all. Especially not the way you claim to know him ... Hypocrite! So you continue to sit year after year, going nowhere. Sleeping on the pew you allow the very religious system that you sit in to rob you of genuine spiritual reality. Satanic Laughter echoes throughout the heavenlies at your plight. "Another One!" void of reality and purpose in the Kingdom of God. Go ahead, sit there in the Dead Sea and Pay your Tithes. The grave awaits you with laughter and open arms!

**When Was the Last Time You Really Heard God?
Jesus Said, "My Sheep Know My Voice."
You Can Hear Him. Your Father Desires To Embrace YOU!**

The first group of church goers at the restaurant has never heard God. The very doctrines and religious traditions that they practice prove that fact. They are sitting in a Total Spiritual Death Trap and a Man Made Evil Illusion. From Maryology ... To the ordination of Homosexuals by the Episcopals surely the members are spiritually dead already! If Martin Luther were alive today he would Rip His Name from that Institution and NAIL a list with 199 Items made by Man! Presbyterians, ... Your wealth consumes you! <u>Reprobate Silver!</u>

The Baptists think they hear God from reading the ink on a page. Someone needs to remind them Faith comes by Hearing, Not Reading. Jesus said you search the scriptures because in them you think you have Life. I Am The Way, the Truth, and the Life! Reading the Bible out Loud Is Not Hearing God! Spit and polished, all dressed up, and not a hair out of place, that is a Baptist. (Perfect Lives that <u>Appear</u> to be in order on the surface). It's that fake smile with ink in their teeth that exposes the Baptist Religious Spirit.

The Charismatics are sure they hear God while they <u>"Robotically"</u> pray in tongues without hearing God's Heart First. Through their abundant speaking, their Religious Vanity is exposed. God would say to them that they need to learn how to shut up and Listen to the Father's heart. Brass cymbals, broken cisterns, empty vapors of vanity, that is a Charismatic. They are "Filled" alright ... with what we do not know yet. They are the Largest Prostitutors of the Gospel ... Just turn on "The Paul and Jan Comedy Hour" and listen.

That Foolishness Is Reality?
Jezebel and Ahab
$elling Jesus for a Dollar!

Is it any wonder that the Image And Integrity of the Church Is Challenged as well as Disgraced daily?

$66,666,6

Help Me Take This Gospel Around The World. Send In Your Pledge and God will Give You a Hundred Fold Return!

Sucking Up For His Own Show!

Is it any wonder the image and integrity of the church is challenged, as well as, disgraced daily? The church was supposed to be the manifold wisdom of God on the earth. Where is it? Our hypocrisy is evident for all to see, shame on us. We are responsible for the desecration of what was to be the most wonderful place on the earth. Wake up; to turn it around it will require that you get off of the pew and out of the grave that awaits you. You will have to find your own Purpose and Destiny. The first thing you will have to do is walk away from the Law and "The Lie of the Tithe."

Let's Examine Jesus' Ministry.

Not One Time
In All of Scripture Will You Find Jesus
Asking Anyone for Money!

You Will Never
Find Jesus Making an Appeal for Money
Or Saying,
"Help Me Get the Gospel out."
"If You Don't Give
This Ministry Cannot Go on."
"I Need Your Help,
Please Do the Best You Can Do."
"If This Ministry Has Been a Blessing to You
Please Send a Donation."
"Help Us Stay on the Air."

Jesus Never said,
"If you go to Church, then that is where
You should Pay your Tithes!"

Jesus Never Taught Anyone How to Make Money. Jesus Never Passed an Offering Plate. He Never Had an Usher! There was no doctrine for church growth. Jesus Never endorsed the theology of cell group ministry. Jesus Did Not tell His disciples to start Sunday school after His departure. Jesus did not give them a paper program to pass out for Sunday morning services.

Jesus Never instituted visitation, except for the Divine Visitation of the Holy Spirit. Jesus Did Not develop a building program for the comfort of people. Above all, Jesus Did Not introduce one-hour services, altar calls, infant Baptism, holy water, sprinkling, religious clothing, or An Offering Plate!

In spite of what the pulpit tells you, Jesus never collected tithes. Jesus never paid tithes. Why is there no record in the New Testament? It would have been a Great Example for us to consider if Jesus Had Paid Tithes. Why did God not have Jesus Pay Physical Tithes? Shame on You! Tithes were not something that were paid. Tithes were eaten! I thought you understood that by now.

The gospel was never commissioned by a single act of the flesh. If the flesh of man could carry out the gospel, then man would be in charge of salvation. Salvation is a gift from God, not man. Today many think that they have encountered God because of some man made emotional appeal from the pulpit. Normally, this appeal comes to you at a desperate time in your life. It could be a family death, loss of job, money problems, divorce, or any number of issues. "Why don't you trust God?" the pulpit will say. Loony Tune Television does that all the time. Trust me, someone is always watching with some kind of a problem somewhere.

If you decided to serve God during a hard, emotional time in your life, Guess What? You do not get in that way! You cannot make a conscious decision to serve God. It is not up to you! The Institutionalized Church is full of twice dead people that think God has redeemed them. Their redemption was by Deception and the Crafty words of men ... who make emotional appeals for membership.

They know that someone attending that day will have a problem of some kind. Have they tricked you? Are you Twice Dead? Twice dead and plucked up, full of head knowledge and religion, but void of Genuine Godly Reality. The gospel has only one agent on the planet! The El Presidente of the Gospel is the Holy Spirit <u>ALONE</u>! If you encountered man and his religious system, you have never encountered the Holy Spirit! If you have been encouraged to walk an aisle at an emotional time in your life, I would seriously doubt the legitimacy of your salvation.

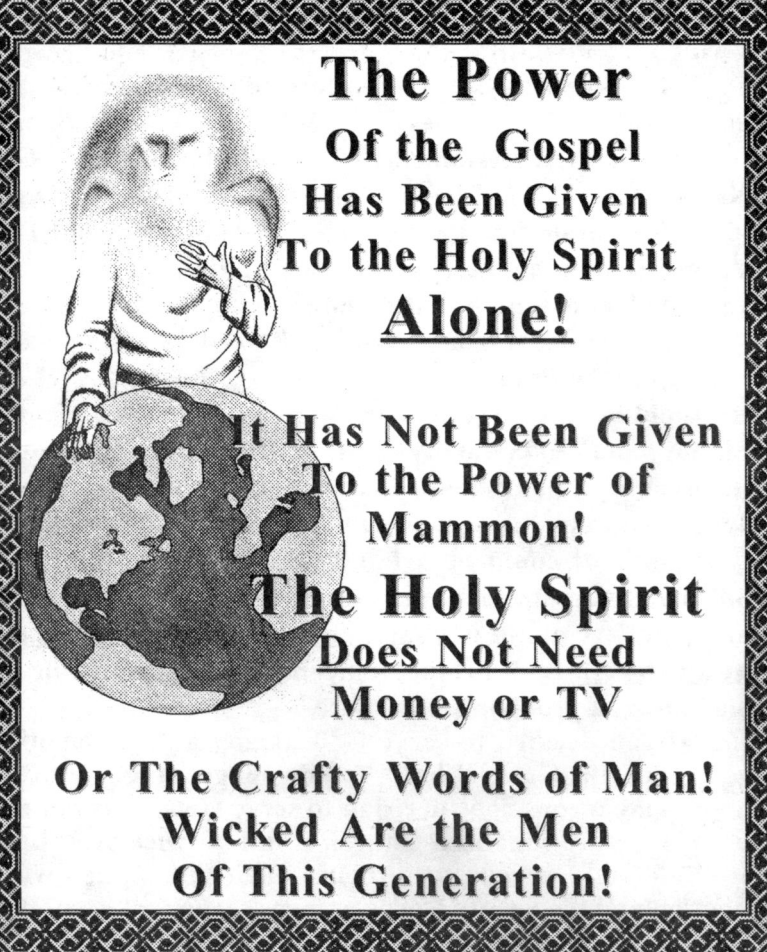

The Power
Of the Gospel
Has Been Given
To the Holy Spirit
Alone!

It Has Not Been Given
To the Power of
Mammon!
The Holy Spirit
Does Not Need
Money or TV

Or The Crafty Words of Man!
Wicked Are the Men
Of This Generation!

Jesus' ministry was evidently so wealthy that The Treasurer Judas Sold the Minister for 30 pieces of silver. We know that money was given because Judas was the designated treasurer. Isn't it ironic that the one in charge of the money would end up being the betrayer? In his entire ministry Jesus never taught anyone how to make money. Scripture clearly proves that Jesus taught the exact opposite. "You cannot serve God and Mammon." "Sell what you have and give it to the poor then come and follow me." "If any man comes after me let him deny himself and take up his cross." **Jesus did use natural examples of physical substances to teach a spiritual lesson.** Please reread that last sentence. Let me encourage you to get the Video Series on the Lordship of Christ.

The natural eyes of today's charlatans will always lead you to a natural understanding of scripture. They will always point out physical substance in order to pervert your faith to pursue natural substance. Many will tell you that you must have faith enough to believe in order to receive something physical from God.

In our study on tithing we have found that you must come to know God as your only sovereign source of provision. No one that pursues God for physical substance of any kind really knows Him. The pursuit of physical substance is what kept the children of Israel in the wilderness for 40 years. If you always relate to God with a natural need for physical substance, I would seriously begin to doubt the legitimacy of your salvation. The pursuit of natural substance by the pulpit and televangelists has reached a disgusting level. On more than one occasion I have heard many speak about the quality of Jesus' robe that was traded by the Roman soldiers at Calvary. In order to prostitute you with their gospel of Mammon, these evil men are willing to desecrate the very clothing that Jesus wore to Calvary. Shame on them! If you could see their spiritual clothing, you would run from the place! Their garments are full of spots, blemishes, and wrinkles.

Let's examine some of the most abused passages in the New Testament today. When you hear someone twist these scriptures in the future, stand up and speak out. Real love will NOT remain silent when it sees Injustice, Heresy, or Hypocrisy. If you choose to remain silent, you are guilty of condoning their actions and speech. You will be held responsible and give account before God about why you remained silent.

The Poor Widow Woman.
Mark 12:41-44

41   Now Jesus sat opposite the treasury and saw how the people put money into the treasury. And many who were rich put in much.

42   Then one poor widow came and threw in two mites, which make a quadrans.

43   So He called His disciples to Himself and said to them, "Assuredly, I say to you that this poor widow has put in more than all those who have given to the treasury;

44   "for they all put in out of their abundance, but she out of her poverty put in all that she had, her whole livelihood." (NKJ)

TREASURY

This is not seed faith planting. This is not giving to get or giving out of your need. Regretfully, most of the time these scriptures are used on people who are at their lowest point in life, in order to provoke them into giving something that they do not have. The preacher or televangelist will tell the viewer that as an act of faith they need to give out of their want. Naturally, they will become the vessel for you to demonstrate your faith on, "As a point of contact with God. Whatever you need put your hand on the television screen as a point of contact." Nothing is more abominable in the sight of God than someone that would intentionally prey upon the poor. There will be a special place reserved for every man that has preached a message of giving to get from these passages. Every message preached by anyone that this woman was displaying an act of faith by throwing into the treasury all that she had will receive judgment in this life. Take heed what you hear! Judgment is coming and it is not for a lost and dying sinful world. Judgment is coming to the Pulpit and the Televangelist! It will surpass the shock waves of Jimmy Swaggert, Jimmy Baker, or another child-molesting Catholic Priest. It will begin severely, and increase in severity until the purifying fire of God consumes all of the religious chaff speaking a word in His name! "Woe to the shepherds!" Many of you will see the purifying fire of God at your Religious Institution. Read Jeremiah Chapter 23 for that day is upon us. We are in the Shadow of approaching Judgment!

Jesus never made this poor widow woman a promise that her act of putting money into the treasury would get her a return on her investment. Remember that offerings were free will. Jesus did not jump out of his chair and say, "Look at this woman. NOW THIS Is What I call $eed Faith Planting!" He did not run up to her and tell her that she had Great Faith. *Faith* *was* *Not* *present* *According* *to* *What* *She* *Put* *In*. Jesus never told the disciples that were with Him that this was the way to prove to yourself that you have Great Faith in God.

$ Faith Was Not Involved! $

The Lesson to Be Learned Had Absolutely Nothing to Do With The Amount That The Widow Woman Put in the Basket!

Jesus pointed out to His disciples that this widow woman knew God more intimately than the others who were in their pride putting in large amounts. In God's eyes this widow woman displayed a heart of love for God more than the rest of those who were standing by the bucket. Jesus spoke about one thing: those who give out of their abundance and those who really know and love God intimately with their whole heart. Jesus was saying, "You see those guys standing over there. They think that they are something else because they put in big money. They are arrogant, prideful, and they do not know God at all." You see, "In the Father's eyes this woman has put in more than anyone. She came willingly and privately within her own heart."

Her very act proved that she knew God deeply and was totally dependent upon Him. This woman knew God as her Sovereign Source of provision! Because she had spiritually come to know God intimately as her sovereign source, she was free from the fear of Mammon and the loss of all things. Her act of putting in her last two mites proves that she had no fear. The tither under the Law would empty his storehouses every three years. This widow woman with her last few cents was emptying Her Storehouse. Mammon had No Hold in her heart or life! It speaks volumes about her total dependence upon God. She was spiritually richer than anyone standing near the bucket was. What fear holds you?

You must realize That God allowed this widow woman To be in that desperate situation So that YOU can learn.

She is not in the book by coincidence. To be poor and a widow must really have been a tough life in her day. Her entire life was for this one example of where you are to come to within your heart. If you really do not know God as your Sovereign Source of all substance and the reason for your existence, you are far removed from Reality. I can hear some of you say that God is your Source. Do YOU Tithe? Few are those who will walk in Deep Intimacy with God.

She did not run around the temple shouting, <u>**"I put my last two cents in, now God has to bless me."**</u> That Mentality and Teaching Is SATANIC! **No, her heart was not haughty and she did not challenge God foolishly! She quietly walked away in her Integrity and Intimacy with God.** Her heart was rich and full with that Intimacy. I pray that you will find that intimacy for yourself. If you do, you will possess what she did. Money cannot buy it and nothing compares with being totally dependent on and knowing God as your Sovereign Source.

If you were there that day, where would you have been standing? Would you be standing with the prideful that were proud of how much they put in? Do you like standing around the offering plate within your heart?

Is there a plaque somewhere with your name on it about your contribution? Are you a Founder Member? Is your heart prideful about what you put in? Do you tithe out of your Convenience or Abundance? Do you make sure that you get your Tax Deduction? Do others know about your "good works?" Do you practice the Law of Tithing because it makes your flesh feel good? You have your reward ... <u>YOUR VANITY WILL BURN UP!</u>

This widow woman is on my personal list of people that I would like to meet. Her obedience gave me an opportunity to understand a genuine deeper reality about God. Her Purpose in the Kingdom touched my heart. It is my personal desire to be found standing among people like her when I arrive home. People filled with Integrity, Honor, Virtue, and an Undeniable Love for God. People who know God intimately as their Sovereign Source. People who found their Purpose and Destiny while they were here. People that did not <u>COMPLAIN</u> about God's provision. Complaining about God's Provision will cause you to wonder in the wilderness all of your life until you Die there. Just Like the Children of God In Exodus!

The widow woman went away the same way she came in. A poor Widow Woman living Life on the Edge with God as her Source. Jesus did not promise her a hundred fold return. I do believe that in eternity she will inherit Spiritual Wealth too vast for human comprehension. Life does not consist of the abundance of "Things."

May the wicked men of this generation receive a full reward in this life and in the life to come for their intentional perversion of the truth.

May you, my friend, "Come out from Among them, and be ye separate" Saith the Lord.

Luke 6:38

> 38 "Give, and it will be given to you: good measure, pressed down, shaken together, and running over will be put into your bosom. For with the same measure that you use, it will be measured back to you."(NKJ)

I believe that this passage is a cornerstone in the giving to get gospel. Normally this scripture is intentionally quoted out of context and by itself. If you read this scripture with a natural eye, you could assume that Jesus was speaking about natural things. Especially if you read this passage all by itself. If you dismiss the passages above and below verse 38, you will miss the entire CONTEXT of what Jesus was speaking about.

Jesus never taught anyone to obtain natural substance. To even Imply that the Son of God did this is Spiritual Witchcraft. When Jesus speaks about men heaping things into your bosom, it has absolutely nothing to do with natural substance. The Son of God was speaking about a Spiritual Reality that was available for you internally. Jesus was speaking about a Spiritual Lifestyle that was available for Everyone on the Planet. This spiritual lifestyle was not just available for those of you who live in Christian City. This lifestyle was AVAILABLE FOR EVERYONE. In all of these passages, Jesus never spoke about money. Jesus certainly never spoke about anyone giving money in order to get money back. He certainly would never endorse a ministry that would use such evil tactics.

The days of Tolerance and Silence about Such Evil Ministries are over!

Life and Spiritual Life
Does Not Consist
In the abundance of natural things.

The spiritual life that Jesus was speaking about in this passage is directly proportional to only spiritual things. Jesus was talking about spiritual conditions within your heart. If you give kindness, forgiveness, fairness, love, and grace from a heart of humility you will receive the same thing back from others. In other words, Jesus gives us another definition of the Golden Rule. How you treat others is how they will treat you.

> **Nothing in your Spiritual Life will Ever Have a Natural Substance attached to it. To find a rich Spiritual Life YOU Must Eradicate your heart of all hypocrisy and Every Lust of the Flesh.**

When we examine the scriptures above and below verse 38, we can learn some very profound spiritual truths. We will see that Jesus is speaking about a whole lot more than having a life full of spiritual realities. You will see that Jesus is speaking about you living a life knowing God as your Sovereign Source. In the end, I hope that you realize this scripture was intentionally plucked out of context for the Evil Benefit of the Speaker.

Luke 6:20-23

20 Then He lifted up His eyes toward His disciples, and said: "Blessed are you poor, for yours is the kingdom of God.

21 Blessed are you who hunger now, for you shall be filled. Blessed are you who weep now, for you shall laugh.

22 Blessed are you when men hate you, and when they exclude you, and revile you, and cast out your name as evil, for the Son of Man's sake.

23 Rejoice in that day and leap for joy! For indeed your reward is great in heaven, for in like manner their fathers did to the prophets. (NKJ)

From the very beginning of these passages, Jesus destroys the giving to get gospel of Oral Roberts, Kenneth Copland, Fred Price, and Kenneth Hagin. The POOR inherit the Kingdom of God. The hungry one day will be filled. Those who speak out in the name of God for truth will receive a reward. <u>**Jesus did not make a promise that when you became a son or daughter of God that you would inherit material riches**</u>. Obviously, you could be poor in Spirit until you inherit the true riches found only in the Kingdom of God. You could also Spiritually Hunger for Righteousness and Truth. Only within the Kingdom will you be filled. Perhaps, your life was full of grief and bitterness, which caused much weeping. When your eyes are opened to the reality of the Kingdom of God you will laugh and leap for joy in the face of adversity. If material riches were to be a Kingdom reality, then Jesus is in trouble with what he says in the very next verse. We will discover that there is a deeper spiritual meaning in the entire context for us.

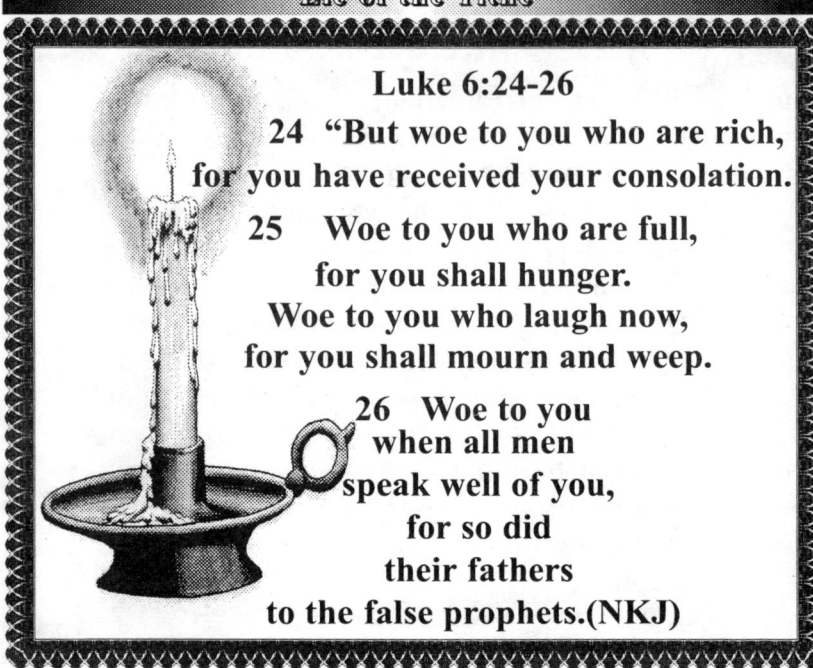

Luke 6:24-26

24 "But woe to you who are rich, for you have received your consolation.

25 Woe to you who are full, for you shall hunger. Woe to you who laugh now, for you shall mourn and weep.

26 Woe to you when all men speak well of you, for so did their fathers to the false prophets.(NKJ)

If Jesus was speaking about giving to get physical substance in our original verse 38, of "give and it shall be given," He sure blows it right here. He warns that the rich have received their reward and they will face judgment. Woe to you that are full! You may have a nice and comfortable life but in the end you will weep and mourn. Why? The only thing that fills the heart of the Rich is PRIDE and GREED! How will you ever explain to the King of Life who gave it all that you failed to see the needs of others. That is why you do not want to hear Him. He will tell you to give it all! Try one day to justify your Christian abundance before Him ... you will not! Learn to hear Him and give to whom He tells you and life will become Alive! A woe is a severe warning. A woe is kind of like the fear that you experienced as a child for doing something wrong. You just knew that when you got home you were going to get it for what you had done wrong.

Make no mistake about it. You will get it.
You can take Jesus at his word.

Many of you foolishly suppose that Jesus is just kidding around about Riches. If you could see what awaits you, you would run from your covetous ways. Materialism and Covetousness will always blind you to the needs of others. A heart that cannot see the needs of others is a Godless heart. I am not speaking about your occasional little Christian do good ditty that you do occasionally to make your flesh feel good. I know of a man that gives away a lot of Bikes and Things to Children. He thinks it is a way to share Christ with his works. They are works alright ... the kind that justifies the Flesh for having Abundance! God sees through that! Covetousness is Idolatry, and you will become Its harlot. Do all men speak well of you? Then perhaps you are not salt and light.

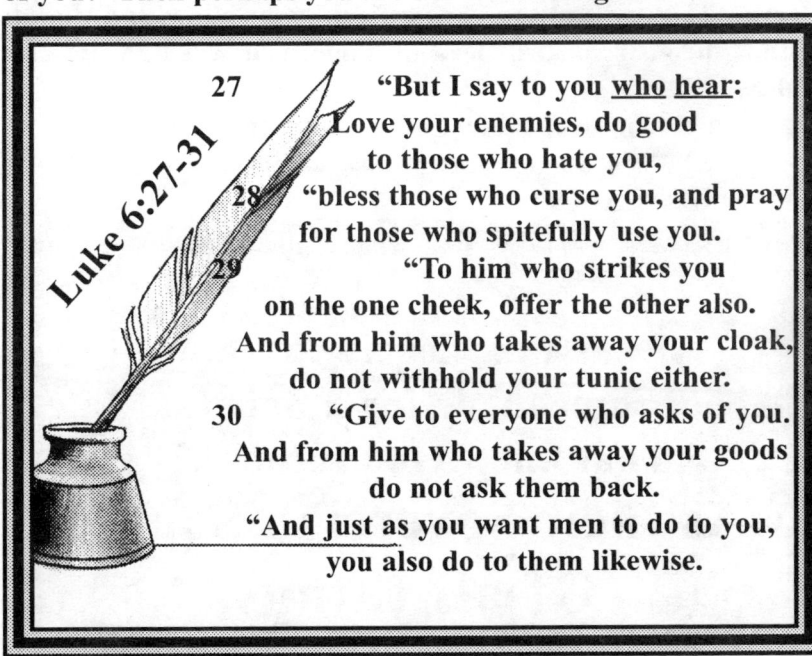

Luke 6:27-31

27 "But I say to you <u>who</u> <u>hear</u>:
Love your enemies, do good
to those who hate you,
28 "bless those who curse you, and pray
for those who spitefully use you.
29 "To him who strikes you
on the one cheek, offer the other also.
And from him who takes away your cloak,
do not withhold your tunic either.
30 "Give to everyone who asks of you.
And from him who takes away your goods
do not ask them back.
"And just as you want men to do to you,
you also do to them likewise.

Jesus seems to miss the point of materialism in verse 38 again by saying, if someone takes away your coat give him your hat also. How could anyone heap anything into your bosom if they took away what you had? Much less, if you were required to give them something else to take with them. The theology of Jesus will not fit into today's theology.

Jesus goes on to proclaim that you are to give to everyone that asks you for anything. Then Jesus really goes way out on a limb when he says, "if someone takes away your goods, do not ask for them back." My, we have a problem. How many people have you failed to get involved with because it could have cost you more than you were willing to lose? Feeling uncomfortable right now? I hope so. Isn't it funny how your wallet and self-preservation dictates the degree of love that you allow to be expressed through your life. Why do you loan something to someone and keep a mental account of when you are going to get it back? What was Jesus really speaking about? I have never found that the words of Christ are easy to digest. They will always be difficult to swallow and digest. Within them, if you will feed on them, you will find life and reality.

In the natural context of verse 38 "give and it shall be given," none of what we have looked at thus far will fit at all. Spiritually, everything will fit.

> # Jesus was clearly speaking
> ## About someone living a Spiritual Life
> ## That knew God Intimately
> # As their Sovereign Source
> # Of all things.
> ## When that becomes
> ## A Spiritual Reality to You,
> ## Nothing will happen in life that can
> ## Disturb you.

You can lose your job, house, car, credit report, and even a family and have peace. God has a witness against you waiting in Heaven. The widow woman is a living testimony against your greed and covetousness. She was capable of knowing God as her sovereign source for all things that pertain to life. What is your excuse? The Father seeks to glorify Himself through your life. If you will seek Him with your whole heart, He will reach through your life to touch others. If you are carnally minded about earthly things, you will remain clueless to this Spiritual Reality. All of these passages speak about someone that knows God intimately.

Jesus Continues to Point Out That This Person Will Be Salt and Light.

Luke 6: 32-35

32   "But if you love those who love you, what credit is that to you? For even sinners love those who love them.
33   "And if you do good to those who do good to you, what credit is that to you? For even sinners do the same.
34   "And if you lend to those from whom you hope to receive back, what credit is that to you? For even sinners lend to sinners to receive as much back.
35   "But love your enemies, do good, and lend, hoping for nothing in return; and your reward will be great, and you will be sons of the Most High. For He is kind to the unthankful and evil. (NKJ)

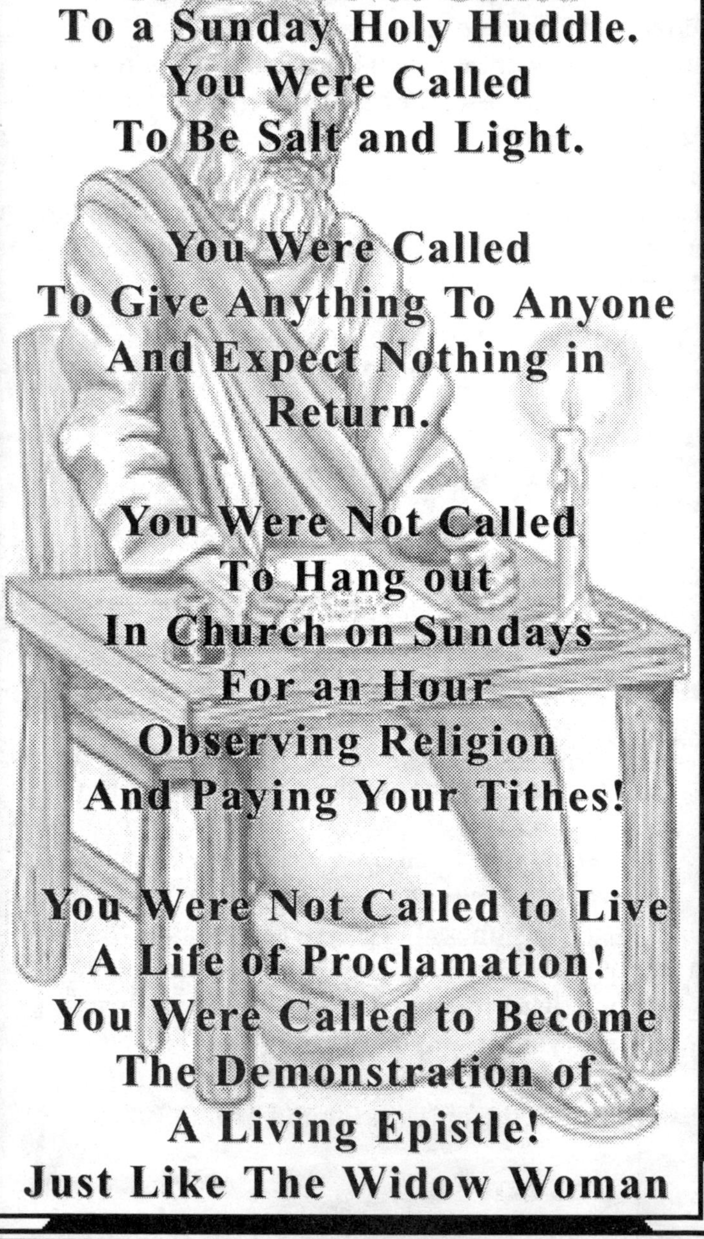

You Were Not Called
To a Sunday Holy Huddle.
You Were Called
To Be Salt and Light.

You Were Called
To Give Anything To Anyone
And Expect Nothing in
Return.

You Were Not Called
To Hang out
In Church on Sundays
For an Hour
Observing Religion
And Paying Your Tithes!

You Were Not Called to Live
A Life of Proclamation!
You Were Called to Become
The Demonstration of
A Living Epistle!
Just Like The Widow Woman

Luke 6:36-38
READ

36   "Therefore be merciful, just as your Father also is merciful.

37   "Judge not, and you shall not be judged. Condemn not, and you shall not be condemned. Forgive, and you will be forgiven.

38   "Give, and it will be given to you: good measure, pressed down, shaken together, and running over will be put into your bosom. For with the same measure that you use, it will be measured back to you."
(NKJ)

Everything proceeding verse 38 emphasizes what you should possess spiritually in your relationships with others. These fruits should be available to those who say they know God, as well as those who do not know God. Nothing in the entire scriptures that we have read even remotely implies that you should be able to give something natural in order to receive something natural. To be carnally minded is death; to be spiritually minded is life and peace. Choose life.

I must point out one other truth contained in these passages. Jesus never taught anyone not to judge. He did teach that we are not to judge hypocritically. If you were not to judge, then how would you discern good from evil? How would you know them by their fruits?

The Pulpit has brainwashed many into believing that you are not to Judge. This is done in order to keep people from Judging what they are doing. The Classic Sign of Any Cult is a unique Ability to take away judgment by its followers. You must judge everything, but do not pass judgment in your own strength. God will administrate that.

If you do not Judge Then how would you know them By their Fruits?

Please take the time to read the following verses where Jesus expounds on how you are to judge.

Luke 6:39-45

39   And He spoke a parable to them: "Can the blind lead the blind? Will they not both fall into the ditch?

40   "A disciple is not above his teacher, but everyone who is perfectly trained will be like his teacher.

41   "And why do you look at the speck in your brother's eye, but do not perceive the plank in your own eye?

42   "Or how can you say to your brother, 'Brother, let me remove the speck that is in your eye,' when you yourself do not see the plank that is in your own eye? Hypocrite! **First remove the plank from your own eye, and then you will see clearly to remove the speck that is in your brother's eye.**

43   "For a good tree does not bear bad fruit, nor does a bad tree bear good fruit.

44   "For every tree is known by its own fruit. For men do not gather figs from thorns, nor do they gather grapes from a bramble bush.

45   "A good man out of the good treasure of his heart brings forth good; and an evil man out of the evil treasure of his heart brings forth evil. For out of the abundance of the heart his mouth speaks.(NKJ)

In verse 41 and 42 Jesus makes it clear that before you correct something in your brother's life, fix it in your own. Otherwise, you cannot help your brother. He speaks about someone judging another hypocritically. You are to judge every word that is spoken to you from a pulpit or over Christian television. Again, I use that term Christian television very lightly. Jesus would say, "Do you smoke?" Then do not judge a smoker. It is really that simple. The blind will lead the blind into a ditch.

Become intimate with God and avoid the blind leaders of our day. Do not end up in a ditch with them. When God delivers you of your personal infirmities, then you can help others. You are not to sit on a pew in the Dead Sea and swallow everything hook, line, and sinker!

Prosperity preachers will always mingle enough truth in their message to deceive you. They know that the blatant exposure of their evil motives will not sell.

Welcome To Another Telethon on TBN
Totally Blasphemous Network

$666,666,666,666,666,666.666

We Need You
To Keep Us On The Air!

Tell them
About Your
Chicken
Honey.

Just send
Money we
need
another
Ranch in
Dallas!

oops

Help Us Prostitute The Go$pel

Everything will sound good for 59 minutes; it's that last minute that you must watch out for. The Holy Spirit Is Never Empowered By Money! The Gospel is only powered by HIM! Write me for a booklet on Judgment that Explains in greater detail <u>YOUR RESPONSIBILITY TO JUDGE.</u>

Especially Such Heretics that appear on TBN,
"The Totally Blasphemous Network!

Jesus Paid Tithes, So Should You.
Have you ever heard that statement?

That Is a Lie!

Matt 23:23-25

23   "Woe to you, scribes and Pharisees, hypocrites! For you pay tithe of mint and anise and cummin, and have neglected the weightier matters of the law: justice and mercy and faith. These you ought to have done, without leaving the others undone.
24   "Blind guides, who strain at a gnat and swallow a camel!
25   "Woe to you, scribes and Pharisees, hypocrites! For you cleanse the outside of the cup and dish, but inside they are full of extortion and self-indulgence. (NKJ)

These scriptures are the New Testament preacher's example that Jesus endorses tithing. That is a lie and nothing is further from the truth. Let me encourage you again. If you have not read Matthew Chapter 23 and Jesus' open rebuke of the Pharisees, you should. You will find that they were not His favorite buddies.

Religion will kill Anyone That threatens its existence. Ask Jesus!

A while back I sent out a number of tithing challenges to numerous churches and televangelists over the Internet. I was offering millions of dollars to anyone who could prove that tithing was a practice of the church from the resurrection of Christ. Although I do not have millions of dollars to give a potential winner, I KNEW IT WAS AN IMPOSSIBILITY.

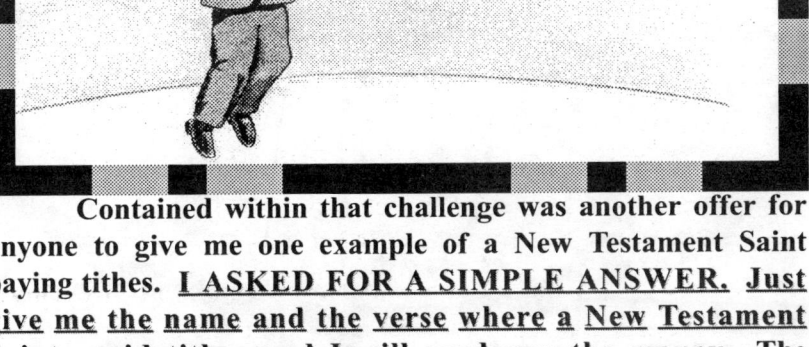

The chance of anyone proving that tithing was a New Testament practice is none, zilch, zip, and zero! The respondents actually stood a better chance at flapping their arms and flying to the moon, than proving tithing was practiced by the New Testament church.

Contained within that challenge was another offer for anyone to give me one example of a New Testament Saint paying tithes. <u>I ASKED FOR A SIMPLE ANSWER. Just give me the name and the verse where a New Testament Saint paid tithes and I will send you the money.</u> The answers that I received from "supposed leaders" only confirmed again just how disgusting they are.

None of them could answer any of my questions. The amount of double talk was astounding. When I told them I was an aging dying man, they really perked up. I am aging every day and one day I expect that this physical body will die. The offers I received from them would astound you. Every one of them was quite shallow in their understanding of biblical hermeneutics. Evidently, most of these men choose to remain intentionally hermeneutically ignorant. Many of them were so interested in the money they proposed to meet with me anywhere so that they could present their argument in person.

Perhaps, they perceived that this dying old man could be convinced in person to leave his money with them. Their wicked hearts were exposed. The passages in Matt 23:23-25 were used by a majority of them to prove that Jesus paid tithes. Repeatedly, I received that statement over the Internet. Coupled with the statement, "Don't you see my friend," Jesus was not against tithing. I assure you I am anything but their friend. Why Jesus endorsed tithing they would say, "See, Jesus told the Pharisees to tithe."

<u>I will agree with that.</u>

THE PHARISEES WERE UNDER THE LAW. THEY HAD EVERY OBLIGATION TO TITHE. YOU ARE NOT UNDER THE LAW!

<u>JESUS CAME TO FULFILL THE LAW. HE WAS SPEAKING DIRECTLY TO THE PHARISEES, NOT TO YOU OR ME. YOU TALK'N TO ME? NO LORD YOU TALK'N TO THEM AGAIN!</u>   To imply that tithing in the New Testament hinges on Jesus' open rebuke of the Pharisees is once again Intentional Deception.

Jesus makes it clear that the Pharisees had missed the boat. They were so intent on observing the natural law that they had missed the deeper matters contained in the law. It is not any different today. The Cheerleaders that contacted me were straining at the tiny physical gnats contained in the law.

Self-Deception Is Denial of the Truth.

It Will always bring Spiritual blindness.

Spiritual blindness will bear fruit after the order of its kind.

The Pharisees had perfected the law down to the smallest detail. In their quest for physical justification, they had swallowed a camel. <u>Blindness, real spiritual blindness, was a result of their gnat straining.</u> They had stared so much at every tiny physical observance of the law that they had become choked by its deception and spiritually blinded. That is why Jesus said that they had swallowed a camel. Self-deception (<u>DENIAL OF THE TRUTH</u>) will always bring spiritual blindness. Spiritual blindness will bear fruit after the order of its kind.

Even the natural eye can easily observe the fruit of that manifestation. Everything will look good on the outside but inside they are full of extortion and greedy self-indulgence. Your natural eyes will not be able to observe the inward darkness of extortion that dwells within them. However, your natural eye will be able to observe their greedy self-indulgent lifestyle. Some are crafty enough to live a low-key lifestyle with a fat bank account.

Lavish living by a minister exposes his inward darkness and extortion. Jesus did not need a Lear jet, Mercedes, BMW, Lincoln, expensive suits, or a television ministry to get out the gospel. Ask yourself. How did God operate before the invention of television in the '50s? We have a warped television mentality. Do you think the Holy Spirit was incapable of redeeming whosoever he called throughout the centuries? All we need are a few men like Moses today. Moses, by the way, did not have a microphone and he led over a million for 40 years.

Spiritual Blindness Will Not See .... That The Pharisees Did Not Offer Tithes In the Form of Money!

Jesus proclaimed, "Woe to you, scribes and Pharisees, hypocrites! For you pay tithe of mint and anise and cummin, and have neglected the weightier matters of the law: justice and mercy and faith. These you ought to have done, without leaving the others undone."

They had paid their tithes probably like most of you. They loved to look good in the eyes of everyone. They had missed the reality of truly knowing God as their Sovereign Source. In their Spiritual Blindness, they had missed the justice for the poor, the hungry, and those who were in sorrow that Jesus spoke about. In their arrogance and pride, they were incapable of showing mercy to those in need. They wanted to appear perfect before others and God by their natural observances. They had become consumed with gnat straining and <u>Tithing After the Law</u>. This blinded their faith until spiritually they had swallowed a camel. **<u>I think if I hear God correctly, there is a lot of gnat straining, camel-swallowing people reading this book.</u>**

Are You Consumed With Tithing After The Law?

Even the Pharisees Never Paid Tithes in
the Form of Money! Tithing was not about
money! You Can Pay Your Tithes and Be Out Of
Touch with God Just like Your Brothers the
Pharisees! If You Tithe You Probably Know God
in the Same Manner As Your Brothers!

Matt 5:17-20

17   "Do not think that I came to destroy the Law or the
Prophets. I did not come to destroy but to fulfill.
18   "For assuredly, I say to you, till heaven and earth
pass away, one jot or one tittle will by no means pass from
the law till all is fulfilled.
19   "Whoever therefore breaks one of the least of these
commandments, and teaches men so, shall be called least
in the kingdom of heaven; but whoever does and teaches
them, he shall be called great in the kingdom of heaven.
20   "For I say to you, that unless your righteousness
exceeds the righteousness of the scribes and Pharisees, you
will by no means enter the kingdom of heaven.

By this time, you should have a real conflict about the
Law. We saw in our previous Chapter of Malachi how the
priesthood was corrupt and responsible for robbing God. We
also found that your pastor intentionally fails to practice all of
the law. We found that he will break into the Law Library and
steal one natural law to use on you. You should have a conflict
with these passages in light of what your church or pastor does
or does not observe.

If Jesus was speaking about the Law
Being observed after the Natural Order of Things,
We would have a BIG BLOODY problem.
We must begin to offer up
Sheep, Goats, and Heifers.

Fortunately, for us Jesus was about to take the law to another level. It was a spiritual one. I do not know anyone that practices the laws of Judaism to this day. Even those who say that they are Jews do not practice the law. Modern-day Judaism is far removed from observing anything after the law. If you observe the Law you Must Have a Sacrifice for Sin. You Must Offer Up a Firstborn or all of your Observances are In Vain!

The church is far removed from practicing anything after the law except for "The Lie of the Tithe." You cannot practice the law without a sacrifice. <u>WHAT WE SEE IN THE CHURCH IS THE THEFT OF ONE LAW.</u> In modern-day Judaism we can observe that they selectively observe natural observances after the law of their choosing. Just Like the Church. The entire practice is void of a sacrifice that was required to bring legitimacy to any natural observance of the law by God.

So what in the world was Jesus saying when He said, "For assuredly, I say to you, till heaven and earth pass away, one jot or one tittle will by no means pass from the law till all is fulfilled." Jesus did not say that the law would not pass away. In fact, he said the opposite. <u>He declared that the law would pass away when everything was fulfilled</u>. What was to be fulfilled? <u>ALL OF THE LAW AND THE PROPHETS.</u>

Jesus said, "Do not think that I came to destroy the Law or the Prophets. *<u>I DID NOT COME TO DESTROY BUT TO FULFILL.</u>*" Every prophecy in the Old Testament pointed to Christ. The law pointed out the perfect sinless sacrifice that was required by God. It exposed man's futility in his quest for right standing with God and his need for redemption. For anyone to assume that the law should pass away <u>BEFORE EVERYTHING WAS FULFILLED IN CHRIST IS A GREAT MISTAKE.</u>

Remember that Jesus was speaking to people Still under the law. Regardless of what Christians say or think, God redeemed people under the law. God redeemed people before the law!

God's Biggest Redemption Came After the Fulfillment of the Law by Christ. Jesus Fulfilled every Law and Prophecy.

Jesus Takes the Law to Another Level!

"For I say to you, that unless your righteousness exceeds the righteousness of the scribes and Pharisees, you will by no means enter the kingdom of heaven." About this time, if I had been standing there thinking naturally I would have walked off hopeless. There was no way that anyone had spent as much time observing the natural laws as the Pharisees had. The great apostle Paul would proclaim about himself "as touching the righteousness, which is in the law, that he was blameless." That is hard to imagine but I will take Paul at his word. Jesus takes the law from a physical observance to an internal spiritual reality. He takes everything from murder, to prejudice, hatred, forgiveness, lust, divorce, adultery, reconciliation, judgmentalism, theft, swearing, hypocrisy, and the list goes on. It would have been very easy for Him to say, "When I finish fulfilling the natural law, you will be called to a higher internal spiritual reality of the law." Let me encourage you to take the time to read all of the scriptures. I would also encourage you to continue straight through Matthew Chapters 6 and 7. <u>The entire purpose of Christ was to fulfill the law and bring you to an internal, eternal relationship with God.</u>

When you read the passages following Jesus' statement about His Fulfillment of the Law on the next pages listen to the proof of where the law was to become spiritually alive.

<u>PLEASE</u> <u>READ</u> <u>THEM</u> and you will know that the Law was to become an internal reality within your heart, not a Physical Observance.

I Had them Printed Just For YOU!

Matt 5:21-48

21 "You have heard that it was said to those of old, 'You shall not murder,' and whoever murders will be in danger of the judgment.

22 "But I say to you that whoever is angry with his brother without a cause shall be in danger of the judgment. And whoever says to his brother, 'Raca!' shall be in danger of the council. But whoever says, 'You fool!' shall be in danger of hell fire.

23 "Therefore if you bring your gift to the altar, and there remember that your brother has something against you,

24 "leave your gift there before the altar, and go your way. First be reconciled to your brother, and then come and offer your gift.

25 "Agree with your adversary quickly, while you are on the way with him, lest your adversary deliver you to the judge, the judge hand you over to the officer, and you are thrown into prison.

26 "Assuredly, I say to you, you will by no means get out of there till you have paid the last penny.

27 "You have heard that it was said to those of old, 'You shall not commit adultery.'

28 "But I say to you that whoever looks at a woman to lust for her has already committed adultery with her in his heart.

29 "If your right eye causes you to sin, pluck it out and cast it from you; for it is more profitable for you that one of your members perish, than for your whole body to be cast into hell.

30 "And if your right hand causes you to sin, cut it off and cast it from you; for it is more profitable for you that one of your members perish, than for your whole body to be cast into hell.

31 "Furthermore it has been said, 'Whoever divorces his wife, let him give her a certificate of divorce.'

32 "But I say to you that whoever divorces his wife for any reason except sexual immorality causes her to commit adultery; and whoever marries a woman who is divorced commits adultery.

33   "Again you have heard that it was said to those of old, 'You shall not swear falsely, but shall perform your oaths to the Lord.'

34   "But I say to you, do not swear at all: neither by heaven, for it is God's throne;

35   "nor by the earth, for it is His footstool; nor by Jerusalem, for it is the city of the great King.

36   "Nor shall you swear by your head, because you cannot make one hair white or black.

37   "But let your 'Yes' be 'Yes,' and your 'No,' 'No.' For whatever is more than these is from the evil one.

38   "You have heard that it was said, 'An eye for an eye and a tooth for a tooth.'

39   "But I tell you not to resist an evil person. But whoever slaps you on your right cheek, turn the other to him also.

40   "If anyone wants to sue you and take away your tunic, let him have your cloak also.

41   "And whoever compels you to go one mile, go with him two.

42   "Give to him who asks you, and from him who wants to borrow from you do not turn away.

43   "You have heard that it was said, 'You shall love your neighbor and hate your enemy.'

44   "But I say to you, love your enemies, bless those who curse you, do good to those who hate you, and pray for those who spitefully use you and persecute you,

45   "that you may be sons of your Father in heaven; for He makes His sun rise on the evil and on the good, and sends rain on the just and on the unjust.

46   "For if you love those who love you, what reward have you? Do not even the tax collectors do the same?

47   "And if you greet your brethren only, what do you do more than others? Do not even the tax collectors do so?

48   "Therefore you shall be perfect, just as your Father in heaven is perfect. (NKJ)

You will never find Jesus
With his hand stuck out looking for money.
You will not find him on the roadside having a church
Garage sale or Washing cars.
He will not be on television asking people for money
So that he can stay on the air.
His spirit will not speak from a pulpit
About Money or Tithing.
You will never hear Him make an appeal
For a building program.
Jesus will never ask you for money to get anything done.
If Jesus needs your money, then He is powerless.
If Jesus needs your money,
Then we must accept Mammon as God.
If Jesus needs your money
Then He is less than who He said He was.
The gospel is free, but if you want to know God
It will cost you something.
Your Flesh!

Under the Internal Spiritual Reality of the Law, I have given you the True Internal Reality about Tithing. You will be responsible for what you know to be truth. You will not be able to offer God an excuse for your shallow relationship.

I Take The Gospel
Around The World.
Money does Not Empower Me.
Christ Our King Directs Me!

I AM Not Strengthened
By Money,
The Pulpit
Or Television!

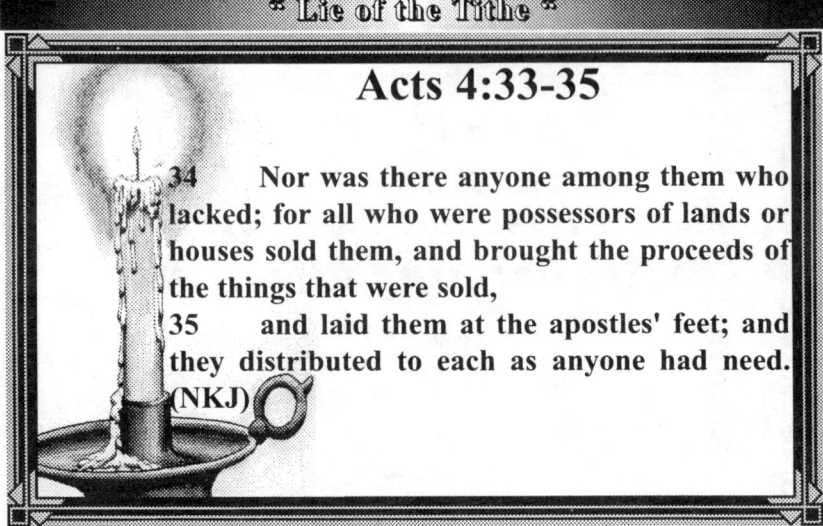

Acts 4:33-35

34   Nor was there anyone among them who lacked; for all who were possessors of lands or houses sold them, and brought the proceeds of the things that were sold,

35   and laid them at the apostles' feet; and they distributed to each as anyone had need. (NKJ)

They all gave and none lacked!

What a witness against everyone or anyone who attends a church on a regular basis! Today, we are so far removed from the reality of what a real church is like; I doubt very seriously that one actually exists. Far too often we rationalize that this is a different day in which we live as the reason for our being so removed from the reality of a true church. **The church of Jesus Christ today resembles a country club or an entertainment center more than a church.**

Like a runner that sets a world record while competing in the Olympics, the standard has been set. An example has been given for every future runner to attain his level of excellence. We, as believers, have a standard of excellence, doctrine, and an inheritance that has been set for us to follow. Our inheritance was not purchased with corruptible things, but with pure holy blood.

NOT ONLY THE PRECIOUS BLOOD OF CHRIST, BUT ALSO THE BLOOD OF MANY MARTYRS AND EARLY CHURCH BELIEVERS WHO WENT BEFORE US AND WALKED IN TRUTH AND LOVE.

If You Truly Mirror The Church of this day, and Examine The Church That Was; Your Heart Should Weep Because Of The Total

Desecration

By Today's Church Of the love and integrity Found In The Early Church.

If you have never read Foxes Book of Martyrs, I urge you to read it. It will build your faith and cause you to examine what kind of faith you have and what kind of faith we see today.

Let's Take the Tithing Challenge a Step Further

I would like to give you another personal challenge from the RESURRECTION of Christ. **I challenge you to go and ask your pastor to find one time in the entire New Testament where a tithe was ever collected for any other reason than a Saint or the Poor.** <u>In every Instance it was used to buy FOOD!</u>
All of the New Testament clearly shows that money was collected for only two primary reasons. The first was for the saints, as we have stated, and the second reason was for the poor. Actually, the entire New Testament does not record one collection for the poor outside of the church; only an admonishment to remember the poor and to do good when you can. <u>Every collection went to the Poor Saints First rather than to take care of the poor within any given community</u>.

If you think that there are no struggling Christians within your city, you are more than blind! We must learn to take care of our own before we reach out to the community in hypocrisy, while there is lack within our own house. Oh no, there goes that food and clothing ministry that gratifies your religious flesh. It is ridiculous for us to think that we can proclaim to anyone, "That We Have the Answer to Eternal Life," when those who are supposedly our brothers and sisters come and go on a weekly basis with basic carnal unmet needs. Oddly enough, this hypocrisy is unseen by most Christian churchgoers; but this common blatant hypocrisy is most obvious to everyone on the outside of the little camp that you attend. And Who Is Blind?

Stop and think with me for a moment about where you attend church today. How many people do you know within your church that have a legitimate need, which remains unmet week after week? You say there are none. Shame on you! If you will take the time to look around your church, you will see the evil manifestations of worldliness draped upon everyone in attendance. The Class distinctions within a church are clearly defined by the almighty dollar. Even a casual observer can see it in the clothing, hats, jewelry, furs, and the praise that is given to the big tither.

Come on! Everyone knows the pastor's favorite ... everyone knows who the big contributor was to the building program. You know the wealthy that sit in your church. Are you the one? Listen to me please. The last place in the entire world where anyone should go away with any lack is a church. This is not a cute biblical story; it is a solid foundational New Testament principle. The real reason that we do not see this principle today is because everyone comes to church with varying levels of covetousness and greed within their own hearts and lives. Leadership has failed to walk by faith, so they cannot lead by faith! Leadership is normally drenched and draped in worldliness setting the example, "Follow Me As I Follow Christ." Yeah Right! Right to the Clothing Store!

I remember back in the '80s when I attended a Jimmy Swaggert Bible conference in Baton Rouge, LA. This was a few years before Jimmy's exposure and God revealed his affinity for prostitutes. I was excited and on fire for God when I arrived in Baton Rouge at his HomeComing Conference. After a few days it was obvious to me that the whole thing was nothing more than a show. From the fake tears to the showmanship of the white waving handkerchiefs, my eyes saw many things. The Holy Spirit opened my eyes and ears to Production Christianity. It was enough to turn my stomach and bring about the deep cry from within my heart again. Please God, I do not want to see anymore.

No one was better than Jimmy at creating an atmosphere of urgency to give money in order to help Jimmy take the gospel to everyone on the planet. "**I need your help, I need you to do the very best that you can do at this time.**" Jimmy always had a new stamp, a new game, or a new gimmick for raising money. In days gone by Jimmy could pack a house. When I arrived in Baton Rouge I soon found out that seating was where the real battleground would be. If you have never encountered "The Look" of Christian Love from the eyes of a <u>SPIRITUAL BAR FLY</u> fighting for its bar stool, you haven't lived. One night I decided to arrive very early, earlier than everyone else did. So early that I never left the afternoon meeting. To my surprise, I found a section right down front that was empty so I quickly staked out my claim; I put my big King Jimmy with my name on it on the seat. I could hardly believe that this entire section was still open! No one had left their books or Bibles on the seats anywhere; there was not another visible claim by a Spiritual Bar Fly anywhere.

My claim was short-lived. As the service was about to begin an usher came up to me and told me that I could not sit there. "These seats are reserved," he proclaimed. As I looked around the auditorium which was filling with people rapidly, I realized finding a seat anywhere inside would be a near impossibility. Luckily, I found a few seats halfway out of the building heading toward the parking lot.

As the service began it seemed that brother Jimmy was suddenly moved upon by the Holy Spirit to interrupt the service and collect money. "I don't normally do this ... but I'm going to obey the Holy Spirit. There are some of you here and the Holy Spirit has been dealing with your heart about giving a large sum of money to this ministry."

The section that I was removed from was now filled with people that were dressed in fine, as well as flashy and gaudy clothing. You know the kind that you see Jan and Paul Crouch wear on TBN. Come on, you know the silver and gold jackets with lots of makeup, jewelry, and hats along with Mr. Businessman from Armani. Although Paul rarely resembles Armani, he is more representative of a <u>Hollywood Cowboy.</u>

Suddenly, a man that now occupied my previous staked out claim, stood up and pledged 25,000 dollars. He was followed immediately by another man seated behind him with a matching pledge of 25,000 dollars, along with an additional 25,000 dollars more. A big frenzy to out give one another overtook that section where I had staked out my original claim. They each continued to stand and out give one another amidst the shouts of "Oh Glory!" from Brother Jimmy as tears, sobbing, and false humility covered him. After this group ran out of ego they stopped giving out of their abundance, and I assure you, they have received their just reward. There seemed to be a long pause of silence waiting to see if anyone else felt moved upon by the spirit.

After a while their contagious prideful ego spread upon someone seated outside of their little group. "Oh Glory!" Jimmy shouted as people seated in the auditorium began to pledge smaller amounts from 100 dollars to 10,000 dollars. The Holy Spirit revealed to my heart the evil workings that were taking place. The Rich were given the seat of the common man in order to run the scam by Jimmy. Do you think that perhaps Jimmy knew who the people were seated in this section? In a few minutes good old Jimmy had raised several hundred thousands of dollars and was shouting "Oh Glory!" and I was sobbing within my heart and shouting in my head ... Oh Bull!

The entire New Testament clearly teaches that everything was done without partiality, class distinctions, greed, pride, or haughtiness. If I were you, I would not scrutinize Jimmy's hypocrisy that closely. Denominationalism is nothing more than racism. I am sure you have a **Few Spiritual Bar Flies** in your church. You know the ones that sit in the same seat every Sunday. The Ones that go to Every Crusade around. Ever meet them? The ones who give you a Christian smile and look if you sit in their spot. Are You One? Some churches put the name on the backs of the pew for brother and sister big shot. Can you imagine the foolishness of churches putting the names of individuals on a pew? If you haven't heard of this, don't laugh, it is quite an old Baptist tradition. Shame on them.

This example of all giving and none lacking in Acts Chapter 4 is a biblical New Testament Foundational Principle. It is not optional or subject to our day and time. Leadership today does not want to practice this foundational principle, much less teach this for obvious reasons. (Power and control.) However, anyone with eyes to see, can see that God was receiving great glory unto Himself, as His children were finally laying everything down for one another in an act of love! The apostle James has some strong admonishments about leadership, giving preference to the wealthy. Do you say you see? Therefore, your sin remains, for if you were blind, you would have no sin.

And they laid it at the Apostle's feet!

And the Apostles picked it up and purchased beach front homes, luxury condominiums, Armani suits, Rolls-Royce's, Mercedes-Benz's, Golden chariots, and had the security of a 401(k) retirement plan, along with a retirement plan from the denominational headquarters. What a sick day we live in. Today, the sickness has the leader of the flock in many cases living behind a fenced in compound with a guard out front.

Why brother ... don't you understand that his anointing is so great that God is blessing him? Find It in the Book! If you are living in a guarded fenced in compound, it is because greed, covetousness, and fear has gripped your heart and not God at all.

The Institutionalized Church
Has been doing business this way For so long that many of you Actually Believe This is how Church Is supposed to be.

You ask me, "How would the pastor live? How would the light bills be paid?" Why brother, you do not muzzle the ox that treads out the corn! True! <u>THE OX IS STILL TO WORK FOR THE MASTER.</u> Today, the Ox is wearing Armani and living a life of financial security with a ring on every finger. Your quick recognition of the too often quoted scripture "Don't muzzle the ox that treads out the corn," shows how well programmed you are. Only one individual is interested in you remembering that analogy. Every time you hear it quoted it is done in order to justify their lusting fleshly desires. But, wait a minute, you say. You don't understand; my pastor is a real man of faith. <u>FAITH IS A VERB, NOT A SUBJECT!</u>

How long will you continue to listen to the endless empty proclamations from the mouth of a trained storyteller <u>WITHOUT WITNESSING</u> The Reality of a Real Living Demonstration from the Pulpit?

The Apostles Gave
A Clear Proclamation
Followed by
A Clear Demonstration!

THEY DID NOT PICK UP THE MONEY. They did not proclaim that God was there because people were coming and money was being laid at their feet. **They did not** shout, jump up and down in a frenzy proclaiming ... "This Is Good Ground Saints, You Had Better Get in on This Deal, Sow Your Seed Here! God is moving right now! Don't miss this opportunity ... if you hurry ... you can get a hundred fold return. Help us take this gospel around the world! Get in on this deal, child of God!"

What a sad, sick, and perverse image this Generation is projecting of the Gospel of Jesus Christ. I declare to you, that in every instance leadership is missing the mark of the prize of the high calling in Christ. They have gone the way of Balaam, "Ministry for a Profit!" All anyone needs to do is look at the lavish gold chairs, the hair styles, and the foolish costumes worn by Jan and Paul Crouch. "Help US take THIS gospel around the world." They are right about one thing ... It's Definitely Their Gospel!

The apostles knew a thousand times over that money would Never be a relevant issue in getting the Gospel out. They knew that Christ had clearly shown them by a living demonstration from His own life that the power of the Gospel was never going to be given over to the Power of Mammon.

"You cannot serve God and mammon."

If you never remember another thing that I say Remember This ... Every time you hear Anyone Stand up in the Name of God and ask for Money
Run from the Place!

"You cannot serve God and Mammon."

This is not some simple little quote to be thrown around. It is a Simple Truth ... to be applied to everyone, no exceptions! You cannot find one comment made by anyone anywhere in the Entire New Testament saying, "<u>If we don't receive your money this gospel message or this ministry cannot go on.</u>" Every time you hear an appeal for money for any other reason than the needs of the saints or the poor, I assure you it is the flesh and pride of man's egotistical personal agenda talking. <u>CERTAINLY, THERE SHOULD NEVER BE A COLLECTION FOR THE POOR OF A CITY IF THERE IS LACK BY ANYONE WITHIN A BODY OF BELIEVERS.</u> This is what the apostles proclaimed in the Book of Acts Chapter 6:4 when they were confronted with the issue of what to do with the money. Their response was, "But we shall give of ourselves continually to prayer, and to the Ministry of the Word." Where are the men who are willing to follow Paul's example as he shouted to everyone, "Follow Me As I Follow Christ."

Let me add a word for those of you that have a Generic all-around down to earth Pastor that does not own an Armani, Rolls Royce, or a Mercedes. If he preaches the law of tithing and benefits in any manner from the collection of tithes, he is numbered amongst the rest. <u>YOU ARE SITTING IN A MAN MADE ILLUSION.</u> He probably does not have the same sales ability or personality type that others may display. Most denominations will have their share of standard generic preachers; ones that are not flashy, have a low-key lifestyle, and everything financially in order in their lives.

When I went to ministry school back in the '80s, I could have gone to the Dallas Theological Seminary. (Dallas Theological Cemetery.) This institution, for most of you who are unaware of it, is the theological assembly line for the Baptist denomination. THE BAPTISTS ARE GREAT AT STAMPING OUT MEN IN THREE-PIECE SUITS WITH A PLASTERED SMILE ON THEIR FACE SAYING, "JESUS LOVES YOU."

This man appears to be just a common looking preacher, nothing flashy, but just as deceptive as any Assembly of God preacher with all of his flash, hype, and handkerchiefs waving. At that time, it was well known that if you completed the course, the Baptist denomination had a church waiting for you somewhere with a starting salary approaching fifty thousand dollars a year with full benefits. I ask you honestly. Is this a man called by God or is this a Businessman? Show me this man in scripture.

Is it any wonder that we have such distant leadership that cannot identify with the needs of the sheep anymore? Remember this. Preachers are the third highest paid individuals in this nation, following doctors and lawyers.

The Entire Religious System And All Denominational Institutions Are Built on One Principle ... The Law of "The Lie of the Tithe!"

Where are the Shepherds with a heart after the sheep? How can we proclaim truth to the lost? We proclaim that we have the right way and still remain nothing more than a religious institution in total hypocrisy to the True Faith of Christ! Any Church Collecting Tithes is Not of the Faith of Christ! Let's face it. Lack is lack, and truly called leadership is what is Lacking within the Body of Christ. TODAY, THE OX AND THE SHEPHERD ARE GOING HOME EATING FAT AND THE SHEEP ARE GOING HOME EATING LIEN.

Tithing Robs You ... Not God, Of an Intimate Relationship with Him.

Remember to send in your Tithes
While you are away
On Vacation This summer.

Some of you need to <u>Keep</u> <u>Up</u>
On your Commitment
Pledges for Our
Building fund.

By the way Thanks
For The Love Offering

The cheerleaders of our day are afraid to release people to hear God for themselves. Why? Because they know that if they do their Man Made Illusion will fall to the ground. Fear and Mammon are their Masters, not Christ. Besides, how can he teach you how to have an intimate relationship with God when he is unable to Demonstrate from His Own Life a Living Biblical Reality Before You?

If Your Pastor Had to Live at the Level Of the Poorest Sheep In Your Church There Would Not Be Any Poor Sheep Very Long!

I venture to say that if this were true your pastor would be out of that three-piece suit in a New York second! He would be down there with his sleeves rolled up among those poor sheep who are struggling in both their faith and finances shouting with a loud voice …

"How Can I Help You?"

THE EMASCULATED LEADERSHIP OF OUR DAY IS FAR REMOVED FROM DEALING WITH THE REALITY OF LIFE AND THE PAIN OF THE POOR SHEEP … JUDGMENT AWAITS THEM. They have failed to realize that God sent the poor sheep; and, in the latter days, they will be a testimony against them. Woe To the Shepherds! God chose the poor of the earth to be Rich in Faith; it is the rich of the earth that are Poor in Faith! This is not a new phenomenon; it was the same in Jesus' day with the Pharisees in the temple. That is why Jesus preached vehemently to them in Matthew 23, "Woe to the Pharisees!"

Every day my heart cries out vehemently, "Lord, deliver your sheep from the hands of ruthless businessmen who have failed to see the needs of your sheep. Deliver your sheep, My King, from the Wicked Men of this generation whose mouths are full of Proclamation Only; *DELIVER YOUR SHEEP INTO THE HANDS OF MEN OF DEMONSTRATION!* "

In my walk through this maze we call Christianity, God allowed me to experience many hardships, heartaches, and heartbreaks in order to form and fashion me for His glory. I can assure you the pain inflicted upon me by the charlatans of this generation not only devastated, but broke my heart, on nearly a daily basis. As a young energetic Christian with a heart full of hope and Thanksgiving for God's wonderful miracle in my life, I never expected such betrayal and corruption to be found in His house.

Many times I cried for hours over the things God would show me. I have cried bedspreads yellow and have crawled for hours on my hands and knees in anguish over what was revealed to my heart by the Spirit of God. At that time I did not know, nor did I understand, what and why God was revealing those things to me. I was unable to comprehend what my Father was building within my heart. Today, I thank Him for every charlatan and every thief He used on me in order for me to deliver this to you. And NO I do not need innerhealing! My life story thus far is in my upcoming book called **Christianity a Hoax?**

I think you will find some very interesting reading from Cover to Cover. This is not a cheap attempt to sell you a book. I really feel within my heart if you will look at what God has shown me and the things that I have experienced, it will open your eyes to the decadence and sickness that breaks our Father's heart. From encounters with Benny Hinn to Jan and Paul Crouch I think You will find some interesting reading. If you visit our internet site on the WWW at SimpleTruths.Net check out the **News video on Benny Hinn's Conspiracy** with the Orange County Sheriff's Office that resulted in my false arrest.

One of the sickest thoughts you can have is that things are this way because times have changed. Walking by faith is never relevant to the times of history or the seasons of life. With over 2000 years of deception working through the hearts of greedy covetous men, <u>I am fully convinced that the enemy controls the pulpits in over 99 percent of all man made institutions that call themselves a church.</u>

The Battle in the Spiritual World Since the Resurrection of Christ Has been over <u>One</u> <u>Thing</u>,
The Pulpit!

God is a God of faith and He only responds to Faith. Any Church that has been built by man, using the old foundational Law of Tithing, is in Total Scriptural Error and resides in the embodiment of the <u>Flesh</u> <u>of</u> <u>a</u> <u>Man.</u> If it has not been built on the foundational principles laid by Christ and the Apostles it is no better than a Social Club. No Other Foundation Can Be Laid; Take Heed How You Build!

In 1984 as a new sheep birthed into the flock by divine intervention, I was less than a one year old believer in Christ when I encountered my first wolf in sheep's clothing. Pastor Charlie Evans was his name at Trinity Assembly of God in Deltona, Florida. Charlie was building a million-dollar church; it would be the biggest church building in Deltona. The amount of rip-offs that I witnessed by Charlie could encompass yet another book entirely. Daily I watched Charlie as he stole, robbed, pillaged and plundered every contractor on the building project. Several times he almost got into a fight with a Jehovah's witness that was working on the project. I begged God daily. Please God, do not show me another thing.

I remember standing in the balcony one day after Charlie had nearly come to blows again with the Jehovah witness. I sat down on a paint bucket stunned at what I had just seen, so I began to ask God. Father, why is Charlie building a church worth one million dollars? Why are we unable to speak to, much less reach this other man? Why Father was there no one available that had enough anointing and understanding from you to speak to this Jehovah's witness? Father, what are we doing?

> What good is a big building Father without Your Presence? Why is it like this?

It was about two days later when God showed up and gave me my answer. I will never forget it!

I was sitting in the balcony pondering the same questions when a loud distinct voice began to explode in my chest.

It Is Because There Are No Priests
In the Temple.
They Are All Businessmen.
They Have Forgotten ... That They
Are My Ministers.
They Are to Minister to Me.
It Is Because There Are No Priests
In the Temple!

What this man would eventually do to my family and myself would be unbelievable. I continued to see many things over the next few months. Charlie would continue to rip me and everyone else off repeatedly.

Several days later I was working in the balcony putting the finishing touches on the hand rail when pastor Charlie walked up to me.

I had put three coats of high gloss polyurethane on the rail and I was in the process of steel wooling and checking the rail for splinters. "How many more coats are you going to put on it?" Charlie asked. It is good enough for my house, so I think that it will work here. I am just checking it for splinters because I do not want a sinner to accidentally get a splinter and to run down front shouting on Sundays. "You might think that you have a live one," I said jokingly. "This isn't your house ... Why, This Is God's House!" Charlie proclaimed. It should get a few more coats than your house.

Then the Holy Spirit Showed up!

I was just a new believer and the Spirit of God put the exact words in my mouth, which would stop Charlie in his tracks. I looked at Charlie directly in the eyes, and the words seemed to come from out of nowhere. <u>"No preacher,"</u> I said, "this is just a building." As my finger pointed at my chest I exclaimed to Charlie, "This Is God's House." All you have here preacher is a building made of wood and stone. I kept my finger on my chest and said again, "No preacher, this is God's house." You have lost sight of the fact that God came to dwell richly in the hearts of men and women everywhere. Stunned, Charlie just stood there with a blank look on his face. Silence hung in the air for what seemed like a few moments and then he just turned and walked away. Everything he was building and everything he was after had been reduced down to the Godly reality of people being the priority and not buildings.

Charlie would go on to build many buildings and a rather large institutional church in the years that followed. Looking back, I suppose the best thing that could have happened would have been for the building to remain empty. The hundreds and thousands of lives and families that Charlie destroyed is amazing.

You name it. Charlie did it! I had only one prayer by the time I departed from Charlie's church. God let me live long enough to see Justice delivered back to Charlie.

The manner in which Charlie did things would come home to him years later. I did not see Charlie again until approximately 14 years later when I returned to Florida.

LITTLE DID I KNOW THAT I WAS ABOUT TO GET AN ANSWER TO A 14-YEAR-OLD PRAYER. Not only would my Father answer my prayer, but he would also place within my hand the very evidence that would lock Charlie up. I ended up turning over a video that exposed Pastor Charlie in such deviate practices that he would eventually plea bargain for three years in prison. It seems Pastor Charlie was spending Tithe Money In Topless Bars as well as running Drugs. I have dedicated well over a chapter in my up coming book "Christianity a Hoax?" to Charlie, and what the spirit of God taught me at the hands of this Wolf in sheep's clothing. You will not believe the things that Charlie has done in the name of God!

Everywhere you look you can see the same thing; church leaders building buildings. Every manifestation of a man's prideful ego at work, making his mark, making a statement, we are the move; God is here! Bologna!! If God was really at our little meetings then why are our cities remaining the same? If the church is the manifold wisdom of God on the earth where is it? Why are there still needs within the body? Big churches, family life centers, schools, day-care centers, and church anytime you want it does not mean God is there! More than likely, it has been built by the ego and the flesh of a well-trained businessman using the Law of Tithing to Justify his Existence.

It is not a move of God when people are taught to give 10 percent of their income from an old biblical law that was abolished by Christ. I don't care how many attend your church on a regular basis or how many you think you are reaching in the name of God. I do not care how many people you feed or clothe! I do not care how many you visit in prison, or how many small children you give a glass of cold water to drink. It does not matter if you can stand a hundred people up who will testify in your behalf about your good works.

If it is built using the Law of Tithing, It stands in the Power of Man's Flesh And Not the Faith of Christ!

Everything that is done or built in the name of Christ, while using the law of tithing upon people as its foundational source of income, is the <u>WORK</u> of a <u>GOAT</u>.

The <u>goats</u> <u>in</u> <u>Matthew</u> 25 <u>WERE</u> <u>NOT</u> <u>the</u> <u>lost</u> <u>as</u> <u>many</u> <u>of</u> <u>you</u> <u>may</u> <u>think.</u> <u>A</u> <u>thousand</u> <u>times</u> <u>No;</u> <u>they</u> <u>were</u> <u>the</u> <u>Religious</u> <u>who</u> <u>worked</u> <u>like</u> <u>a</u> <u>goat</u> <u>in</u> <u>the</u> <u>Traditions</u> <u>of</u> <u>Man</u> <u>and</u> <u>could</u> <u>not</u> <u>see</u> <u>the</u> <u>needs</u> <u>of</u> <u>the</u> <u>Real</u> <u>Sheep</u> <u>in</u> <u>front</u> <u>of</u> <u>them.</u>

Extremely Serious Is Your Reading of Matthew 25

A religious goat according to Jesus could not recognize the needs of his brother or sister or who his brother or sister was. As a religious goat, he was doing work that was pleasing in his own eyes. <u>A RELIGIOUS LEADER GOAT</u> will always try to justify his existence with lots of programs, out reaches, and many activities to keep the attending religious goats involved in a false feeling of purpose. A goat will always have one common manifestation; his heart will always be blinded to the true needs of his brother. That is why the goats responded to Jesus in Matthew Chapter 25:44. "When did we NOT Minister unto you?" The goats never learned who the real sheep were or how to do unto the least of these my brethren. Read it and perhaps your eyes will be enlightened. Jesus told the goats, "Depart from me you workers of iniquity; I never knew you!" You can brag all you want about your fleshly acts of love to the homeless and the poor in your community. Get your pastor, stand him behind the bully pulpit and let him brag about all the good works that takes place on the inside and the outside of your church. Come on! Brag about your food pantry! Do You Tithe? GOATS! FLESH! If you thought the goats were the lost people of the world, can you imagine what else your Lead Goat has taught you in error? Follow Christ and the Apostles, not man! Let Christ show you who His sheep are and minister to them. Let Him have lordship over mammon in your life; allow Him to build through you what He wants. Do you know Him that intimately?

Matt 25:33-46

33   "And He will set the sheep on His right hand, but the goats on the left.

34   "Then the King will say to those on His right hand, 'Come, you blessed of My Father, inherit the kingdom prepared for you from the foundation of the world:

35   'for I was hungry and you gave Me food; I was thirsty and you gave Me drink; I was a stranger and you took Me in;

36   'I was naked and you clothed Me; I was sick and you visited Me; I was in prison and you came to Me.'

37   "Then the righteous will answer Him, saying, 'Lord, when did we see You hungry and feed You, or thirsty and give You drink?

38   'When did we see You a stranger and take You in, or naked and clothe You?

39   'Or when did we see You sick, or in prison, and come to You?'

40   "And the King will answer and say to them, 'Assuredly, I say to you, inasmuch as you did it to one of the least of these My brethren, you did it to Me.'

41   "Then He will also say to those on the left hand, 'Depart from Me, you cursed, into the everlasting fire prepared for the devil and his angels:

42   'for I was hungry and you gave Me no food; I was thirsty and you gave Me no drink;

43   'I was a stranger and you did not take Me in, naked and you did not clothe Me, sick and in prison and you did not visit Me.'

44   "Then they also will answer Him, saying, 'Lord, when did we see You hungry or thirsty or a stranger or naked or sick or in prison, **and did not** minister to You?'

45   "Then He will answer them, saying, 'Assuredly, I say to you, inasmuch as you did not do it to one of the least of these, you did not do it to Me.'

46   "And these will go away into everlasting punishment, but the righteous into eternal life."(NKJ)

So many religious leaders have built programs, buildings, family life centers, and a horde of activities all to entertain us and make us feel as though God is there. None of this stuff will draw you closer to God. Yes, we have the answers to eternity, life, health, and prosperity. That is why many of you have had bake sales, car washes, festivals, and church garage sales to show the world you are the children of the Kingdom! <u>How foolish!</u> <u>GOATS!</u> Who put you on the side of the road in the name of God chasing mammon? Oh, I see. You are the chosen, the children of the Most High. The lost of the world are looking for a Real Demonstration of love, not the kind produced by Smiling Religious Goats. Spiritual Blindness Is the Inheritance of a Religious Goat. Everything they do in the name of God Makes them FEEL Good. A Goat cannot Hear the Master because they cannot See The Real Sheep. However, take heart if you are a Tithing Goat ... One Day you will Hear The Master Speak "Depart From Me ... I never knew You!" Keep on Tithing and doing your Good Works! <u>Learn to Hear Him Who Is Alive and desires to Show You His Sheep, Not A Building Built by the Flesh of Man. Then You will come ALIVE!</u>

Spiritual Blindness
Is the Inheritance of a Religious Goat.
A Goat <u>CANNOT HEAR</u> the Master
Because they cannot See The Real Sheep.
<u>Learn to Hear Him Who Is Alive and desires to Show YOU HIS Sheep!</u>

I venture to say there are few pastoral businessmen that can release you, much less teach you, how to hear God for yourself in what you are to give and where you are to give it. The reason? They do not know how to hear God for themselves. They cannot give what they do not have. This is why they practice the Law of Tithing; it is safer and more secure for them. Let's face it. If you cannot hear God in the carnal realm of what to do with your money, you cannot hear God at all.

It Is up to You
To Enter This Relationship With Your Father.

<u>You</u> Are Responsible For Performing His Will Within Your Lifetime.

* It Is Not*
Between You,
Your Local <u>Guru</u>, And God.
It Is between You and God Alone!

Tithing has always been about communion with the Father. Do not let your left hand know what your right hand is doing. Do not do your alms before men; do them in private. I urge you to enter this fascinating, exciting, reality of God that few will ever experience. Let God build through your life what He wants.

<u>BECOME A TRUE SHEEP.</u>
<u>WALK AWAY FROM THE GOAT HERDER!</u>

It would amaze you to know
The number of men that stand and speak

Sunday after Sunday with a sermon
Prepared by someone they don't even know.

CD Jesus!

Nowadays, you can order all of your sermons for a year on a CD, complete with an outline and jokes. Have you ever noticed how you will hear the same message on television that you heard at church? Do you think this is odd? Later, you will hear the sermon again on the radio or somewhere else.

This is not the Holy Spirit speaking. It is the latest Hot Topic from a CD sermon writer. I am sure that every reader of this book has heard on several occasions a sermon that touched your heart.   More than likely some professional writer prepared it somewhere. In most cases, your pastor never even studied the message until the night before or the morning that the message was given. <u>This is how they advertise the CDs.</u>

"Why spend countless hours studying for a one-hour message? It's all here, you can enjoy the week, and still be ready for church on Sunday morning." The CD comes complete with jokes and funny little stories. Surprised? Not my pastor you say. BULL! Don't be so sure. <u>I say to you if he was hearing God, he Could Not preach the Law of Tithing to You.</u> I assure you that most of the sermons that you have heard could just as effectively been delivered by an electronic mannequin Disney Style. Playing Every Emotional String Within You!

So You Want Proof!
(I thought you would never ask.)

If you have attended the same place for any length of time, you probably can recognize that after a while you begin to hear some of the same messages repeatedly, or perhaps, a slight variation. I'm sure that by now you can tell some of the pastor's personal stories and jokes yourself.

How many times have you heard the same story? How many times have you heard the same message? Oh I get it; God has nothing new to say. Do you find yourself doing the head bobbing special on the pew? <u>Head bobbing and heavy eyelids are proof that the culprit in the pulpit is asleep in his relationship with God.</u> The same old sermons, the same old stories are proof that the culprit in the pulpit is not hearing anything from above. How can anyone deliver a Real Word From God and you fight staying Awake? Why can't you put this Book Down? Why does this Book compel you to read it in spite of your Religious Anger over the exposure of your falsehoods? Become Angry with the Liar that Preaches Tithes to you! If you continue to deny the Truth about yourself and your Little Religious Country Club, you will continue to do the Head Bobbing Special weekly on the Pew ....

Maybe You Should All "Take Up A Tithe" And Buy Your Cheerleader A New Sermon CD.

Oh I can hear each of you saying again … not my pastor! Wanna bet! Does he preach Tithes? Bitter and Sweet water cannot flow from the same vessel. Neither Can Grace and Law! He will deny it, but in nearly every instance someone else wrote the sermon you Hear on Sunday! Talk About Out of Touch or What?

IF he is a Man of God he will be capable of Delivering a Real Word to You. Well over 90% of the Pulpit Puppets get their sermon from a CD, <u>or it is written by someone in your Denominational Headquarters.</u> It is sent to your Pastor so that he can, "LIKE A PARROT," repeat it to you. This is a Man of God? Is this man Hearing God and Speaking on Relevant Spiritual Issues Where YOU Are in Life? What does a CD or a sermon writer know about you?

<u>Of course, your Pastor will deny this Fact.</u>
<u>If He Collects "Tithes" from YOU,</u>

Who Do You Think
Told Your "*Polly Want a Cracker*"
To Do THAT?

Get The Tithe!
We Need The Tithe!
Headquarters Said
"Get The Tithe!"
We need The Tithe!
Headquarters Said
"Get The Tithe!"

Please do not let that Religious Spirit of pride about your pastor and the Holy Huddle you hang out with cloud your vision in beholding the truth. For too long <u>The Voice of Godly Discernment</u> has been sacrificed to the fear of offending. I will not fear offending you and your Religious Pride in order that you might hear the Voice of Godly Discernment. Be Free!

They All Gave and <u>None</u> Lacked!
The Apostles <u>DID NOT</u> Pick It Up!
It was distributed to everyone
That had a need!

God was receiving Glory unto Himself because for the first time His Children were walking in Faith towards God and Love towards one another. Again, I must ask you, are there needs within you Church? Are there vivid Class Distinctions? None, you say!

Look around the parking lot at the cars and you will see the need and the Class Distinction. By the way, the next time you attend a Prosperity Crusade Look at the Cars and you will see that the Prosperity Gospel is a Hoax. If Sowing and Reaping was a Spiritual Reality that "Worked" then "Oral Cancer" and Richard (No Shadow) Roberts would have taken over the World's Money Supply By Now!

Pick Up Every Word And Get Out Of Town Oral!

Early in our study I made a statement that tithing was about communion with the Father. I would like to prove to you that is exactly what was taking place in the early church. It is very dangerous for you to read this book and dismiss the truths that are found within it. You will be held accountable for what you hear and know.

This book is not just another issue for you to talk about during <u>Church</u> <u>Chat.</u> This book is about a Very Evil Religious Root that must be removed from YOUR HEART and the Church. I promise you that every time you attend church from now on, your eyes will see increasingly more truth. In time, if you will not harden your heart and return to your old ways, Your Faith will finally come alive and <u>You</u> <u>Will</u> <u>Find</u> <u>Purpose.</u>

> ## <u>Do</u> <u>not</u> Remain A Goat!
> ## Do Not Remain A Spiritual Bar Fly!
> ## Are you one?

Do you have Your Own Seat at church? Do you have the latest CD's or Video's? Do you need the latest Praise and Worship Music to Worship God? Do you attend every Crusade around? Ever Get Or Give Someone A Look Over A Seat? Are You Filled With Preacheritis? Are You Always After "The Anointed" Cheerleaders? Tithing Makes You Feel Good? Like to be Near "The Pastor?" Do you Crave Spiritual Recognition? Do you Like Doing Good Deeds?

> ## Are You an Usher?
> ## Then Get A Job In The Theater!
> ## Never Mind, You Already Have One!
> ## Would you Please Show
> ## S.B. Fly To Her Seat!

If You Will Not Listen To This
Living Man ...
Then Let the Dead Man Speak!
Ananias Must Have Been
At Least a 50 Percent Tither.

Acts 5:1-5

1   But a certain man named Ananias, with Sapphira his wife, sold a possession.

2   And he kept back part of the proceeds, his wife also being aware of it, and brought a certain part and laid it at the apostles' feet.

3   But Peter said, "<u>Ananias, why has Satan filled your heart to lie to the Holy Spirit and keep back part of the price of the land for yourself</u>?

4   "<u>While it remained, was it not your own? And after it was sold, was it not in your own control?</u> Why have you conceived this thing in your heart? You have not lied to men but to God."

5   Then Ananias, hearing these words, fell down and breathed his last. So great fear came upon all those who heard these things. (NKJ)

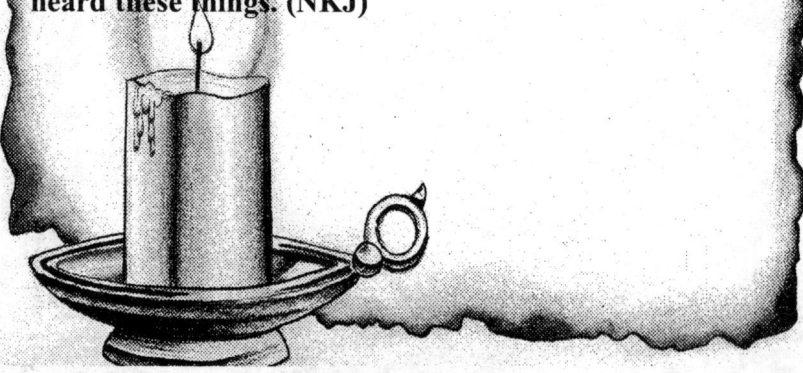

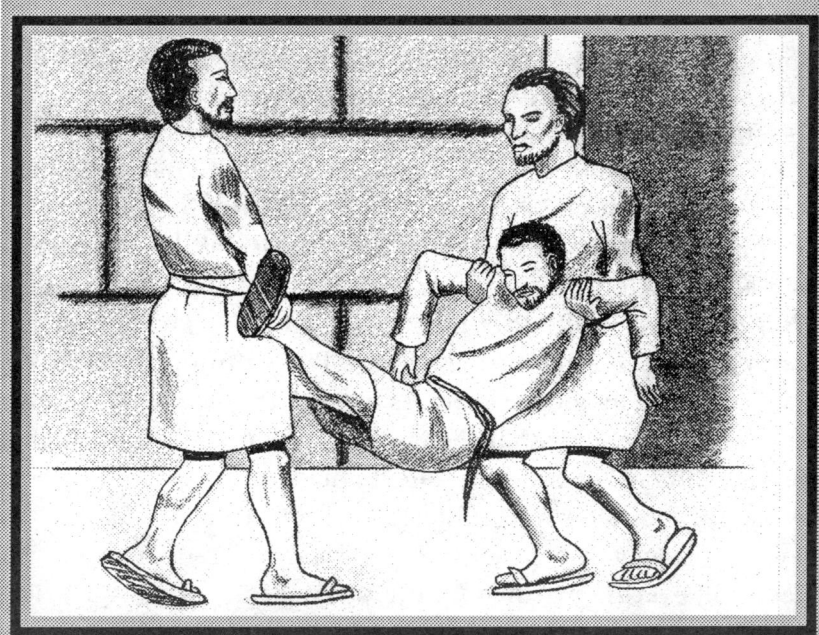

Let's take a close look at why Ananias was struck dead. My concern is that many of you will continue to think the story of all giving and none lacking in Acts Chapter 4 is still just a nice story. An even greater concern is that you might think that this principle was <u>For</u> <u>Then</u> <u>and</u> <u>Not</u> <u>for</u> <u>Now</u>. You may still be of the opinion that times have changed and this is not that way God does business in the day in which we live. That would be the typical answer from the pulpit. God has not changed!

Faith, as I have said before, is not relevant to history, time, or the seasons of your life. Besides, how many times have you heard your pastor say, "God Changes Not." It is extremely dangerous to develop a theology that dismisses Relevant Faith Issues by diminishing them by using the "process of time" as an excuse. To dismiss Issues of Faith with the thought process that God does not do business that way today would mean that God did things in error throughout the book. **<u>IN</u> <u>THIS</u> <u>INSTANCE,</u> <u>GOD</u> <u>WOULD</u> <u>HAVE</u> <u>TO</u> <u>APOLOGIZE</u> <u>TO</u> <u>ANANIAS</u> <u>FOR</u> <u>HIS</u> <u>DEATH.</u>**
Think with me. God would have to apologize for administering His Death Sentence on all of the children of Israel in the wilderness because they failed to relate to God by Faith Alone. God ONLY Responds To Faith In the Life of A Believer! There are serious repercussions for Failing To Respond To Your Father BY Faith!

Jesus would have to apologize to the Pharisees for His scathing open public rebuke of their inability to relate to God by faith in Matthew 23, "Woe to the Pharisees!" I could go on and on with God's displeasure with those who did not relate to Him by faith. While it is true that God does not do business today the way He did business in the Temple (<u>after</u> <u>the</u> <u>Deeds</u> <u>of</u> <u>the</u> <u>Flesh</u>), He no longer requires us to offer a red heifer for sin. You must remember that the law was added until that which is perfect came. The law was added and exposed Israel's, as well as, the practitioner's inability to relate to God by Faith. The law heightened the practitioner's need for redemption. No flesh will ever be justified by the works of the law. What does this say about you if you Practice the Law of Tithing?

If the law had the ability to justify anyone, God would never have sent Jesus. Jesus would never have prophesied that not one stone of the Temple would be left standing. (Matthew 24.) Jesus Himself declared, "Tear it down!" If the Son of God abolished the Temple and destroyed the existing Religious System with His own blood all because of their religious inability to relate to God by faith, what does that mean to you? How offensive do you suppose it is to God for you to dabble in the law? About this time, you should be asking yourself. Do you really know how to relate to God by Faith Alone, apart from the Law? What do you suppose is Jesus' opinion of Your Desecration of His Blood that Purchased Your Freedom from the Law? Do you really want a closer relationship with Him? Then stop Desecrating the Completed Work of the Cross by Your Desecrating Offensive Acts of Tithing and dabbling in the Law. Will you continue in this dead way?

Let the Dead Man Speak!

The question is: why would God administer such severe punishment to a man and his wife over money? After all, Ananias like many today was at least putting something in the basket. I ASSURE YOU THAT EVERY TITHE-COLLECTING PREACHER OF THIS GENERATION MUST ENDORSE AND EMBRACE ANANIAS'S ACTIONS WITH OPEN ARMS! DO NOT LET THAT GET BY YOU!

What are you going to do with Ananias and his death? He was well past the 10% legal mark ... more than most today. The ministers, if you can call them that, not only Embrace Ananias's behavior, it is obvious they also Build Him in YOU.

Instead of Teaching You How to walk by Faith with your Father; YOU, my friend, are $ubtly Taught To Practice Ananias's Behavior.

** Just Listen **
To The Voice ...
Have you Heard It?

"I want to thank those of you who faithfully give to this ministry." "I want to encourage those of you who are behind in your giving to get back on track and trust God." "You cannot out give God." "You know only about 20 percent of the people tithe all the time. Is that you?" "If you do not tithe you are not really trusting God." "Tithing is obedience to what the word teaches." "When you mature in faith you will start to tithe." "God loves a cheerful giver." "Some of you are falling behind in your building fund pledges." "We want to thank Mr. and Mrs B. Fly for their Giving." "I have never met more kind and Giving People than the B. Flys." Don't make <u>ME PUKE!</u>

The Following Statement is the Most
Un-Godly, Un-Church, Un-Kingdom of Christ
Statement of them ALL!
"Will The Ushers
Please Come Forward."

How many times have you heard statements similar to these from the pulpit? Ananias is under construction within you and you do not even realize it!

Why didn't Peter proclaim any of the above statements as a Truth to Ananias? It just does not fit, does it? "We at Apostle Headquarters want to thank Brother Ananias and His Wife for their wonderful gift." I cannot imagine the Great Apostle Peter Ever Patronizing, or Embracing Ananias, can you?

Oh I get it; Peter was unable to see as clear as your preacher claims to see today. Who are you kidding? A 50% tither would be having dinner at the Pastor's Home the Same Night. I am sure that you could write your own list of manipulating statements that you have heard from the pulpit.

Today they are fully equipped, Armed with a *$ubtle Deceptive smile*, TheyAre Masters At Using the Tools OF Manipulation, Condemnation, And Guilt As Ananias is Built IN YOU!

They inflict, endorse, and build the theology of Ananias in the hearts of the people. Some are blatant! Most Are Subtle Innuendoes spoken from the mouth of The most subtle beast of the field, the same serpent found in the Garden of Eden. They are twisting $cripture for their benefit! Shame on them!

How much of Ananias's life has been built within your life from the pulpit? You must realize the extreme importance of Ananias's death and its relevance to you.

I will say it again. Every preacher collecting Tithes must Endorse and Embrace Ananias with open arms! Are you one? Do you Tithe? Are you embraced and accepted with open arms? God did not endorse or embrace Ananias's actions. Let me repeat myself again. Tithing has never been about money!

The issue is your faith and the theft of it.

I suppose you think that the people who were coming and laying money at the apostles' feet were acting out of their flesh. Let's face it. If you have been tithing for any length of time, you are operating out of your flesh. Or maybe you think this was God's way of raising money to establish the early church. If you have been programmed correctly, it is natural for you to think like that. **Listen to Some More of Your Subtle Programming!**

"After all, it's your church, you should get involved in the building program." "Make sure you fill out your pledge cards and turn them in weekly along with your regular tithes and offerings." "We need you to give at this time, over and above your tithes." "Some of you are a little behind in your pledges." "Remember, this is good ground." "We need you to do the very best you can do." "If this is your church, then this is where you should pay your tithes." "This place will become an outreach to the community." "For your convenience your new tithing envelopes now have a number on them; please refer to that number when contacting the office about your tithes."

Yes, my friend, Ananias is alive and well. He Stands in the Pulpit And Tragically, He has been $ubtly Built Within **Your** **Heart**.

Every statement is a falsehood, unbiblical, and filled with The Desires of Man's Flesh. Each statement is nothing more than filthy rhetoric from mouths of men who are out of touch with God. Why can't you imagine any of the Apostles making any of the above statements? Why is the entire Bible Totally Void of such Evil Comments? Yet, you have allowed yourself to become so programmed by the Subtle Masters of our day; that you will sit week after week and listen to this filthy swirl ... believing this is how church is supposed to be. It is not!

Again, the death of Ananias is not some cute little story. It is a prerequisite, an endorsement of a New Testament Foundational Principle. You will not find this foundational principle violated anywhere in the New Testament from the Death of Ananias. Ananias would become the defining line between sheep and goats. The sheep in Acts Chapter 4 as we can see were in total communion with the Father. Everything that was being done was Totally Orchestrated by the Holy Spirit. Each person that sold houses, lands, worldly possessions, or emptied their bank accounts did so because they were <u>Hearing God</u>. <u>They were in communion with the Father!</u> ***Even Ananias was in communion with the Father; he was Hearing God. What about YOU?***

How jealous is God about His children that walk in love and communion with Him? <u>**Ask Ananias ... Can You Hear The Dead Man Speak?**</u> The children of God were in total communion with the Father about what to do with their Worldly Possessions. They were walking in love and harmony with one another for the first time.

Ananias, the 50 percent tither, enters bringing that old greedy <u>Tithing Goat Mentality into this Atmosphere.</u> God was very jealous about what was happening here. It is also evident from these passages that the first priority in the Father's Heart was to teach those who had <u>excess</u> <u>worldly</u> <u>possessions</u> ... to care for those who had any Lack in their Lives. This was done by A Living Demonstration, not another Proclamation. When we allow the Father to have full control over our Worldly Possessions He Will Build What He Wants in us, as well as, what He wants in the world. <u>Can you imagine a</u> <u>church where Christ as the head built what He wanted, instead</u> <u>of man?</u>

This is <u>NOT</u> Theory.
This is <u>HOW</u> it is Supposed to be!

"I will build my church!" Jesus said, "and the gates of hell will not prevail against it!" How true, in a desperate hour, he will raise up A Voice ... Not another Echo of Men.

How long will you continue to sit in silence and unreality? Will you remain trapped in the same religious state as a dead Ananias? Will you be afraid to tear down what man has built in your life and heart so that you may find ... True Reality in Christ? How long will you continue to listen to the $ubtle comments from the pulpit and remain silent? "Will the Ushers Please Come Forward?" Where were the Ushers in Ananias's day? I bet that Ananias wishes that he had been the Head Usher that day. Poor Ananias, if he had only been born in our day, he would have been an okay Joe. Why he could have been an Usher, a Door Greeter, a Sunday school teacher, a Visitation Worker or better yet ... <u>YOU.</u> I think his best job would have been an Altar Worker, since that seems to be where he found his Purpose and Destiny. At least Ananias found His! <u>God put him there for you to see.</u> Do you See? Can You Hear the Dead Man Speak? "Learn To Hear and Obey God Rather Than Man or Your Own Wicked Heart! Do Not Ever Tithe Again!" Can You Hear Him? Don't do it ... Learn to hear and obey God from your heart ... not man!

Today, everywhere we look all we can see is man's agendas. I submit to you that if your building program were genuinely a move of God, a few 50 percent or less tithing Ananias' would have been struck dead somewhere along the way. The simplicity of understanding what happened to Ananias proves that God is not amongst us. Most sit in a Man Made Illusion, <u>TOTALLY UNAWARE</u> that it is one, <u>hence, the definition of spiritual blindness.</u> "Having eyes to see, yet not seeing; having ears to hear, yet not hearing." Wake up from your sleep and rend your heart, not your garments or your wallet. Repent!

Peter made it clear that Ananias fully knew what he was doing. Peter also made it clear to Ananias that he knew that the entire matter of the people coming and giving was being totally orchestrated by the Holy Spirit. Just the questions alone that Peter asks Ananias proves that Ananias was aware of what was taking place. I believe the only conclusion that we can come to is that Ananias had to have asked the Holy Spirit about what to do with his land. At that time, the Holy Spirit told Ananias exactly what to do with the land. If you will go back and read the questions asked by Peter, there is much revealed.

I also find it Very Interesting That Peter Attributed Satan As Being the Spirit Responsible For Bringing That Filthy Greedy Tithing Mentality Into the <u>REAL</u> Church.

If this is true, which I believe it is, then whom ... do you listen to? Who has taught you how to Tithe? Who got you to contribute to the building program of a man? Do you have a pledge card ready, along with your tithing account number? Do they mail them to you directly? Do you deduct your tithes from your taxes each year? Oh I understand; you are led by the Spirit of God! You are in communion with the Father; you know what He told you to do with your finances. Hypocrite!

If you are a religious tither, I can assure you, that you live with this mentality. You always keep account of everything coming into your life to make sure God gets His part. Once again, God does not need your money. Where He is it is of no value to Him. What He wants from you is His right to live and reign in your heart.

<u>It is important to understand why Peter reminded Ananias that everything was still within his power when he owned the land.</u> While it remained, was it not yours? After it sold, was it not your own to control? In other words, you could have kept the land and you could have kept the money after you sold the land. But you sought God, got an answer, and failed to do what you were told. Faith comes by hearing and hearing by the word of God. You heard Ananias, you had communion, and you failed to obey the word spoken to you. The entire book speaks about people who heard God and failed to obey Him. Faith and obedience cannot be separated; it is a two sided coin. If God was really in attendance at your little man made gatherings like you think, there would be many bodies of the modern-day Ananias' being carried out on a regular basis. Oh, I understand, you think this is just a story. Perhaps, according to your thinking, God owes Ananias an apology for his actions. **Ananias is not going to get one and neither are you. GOAT!**

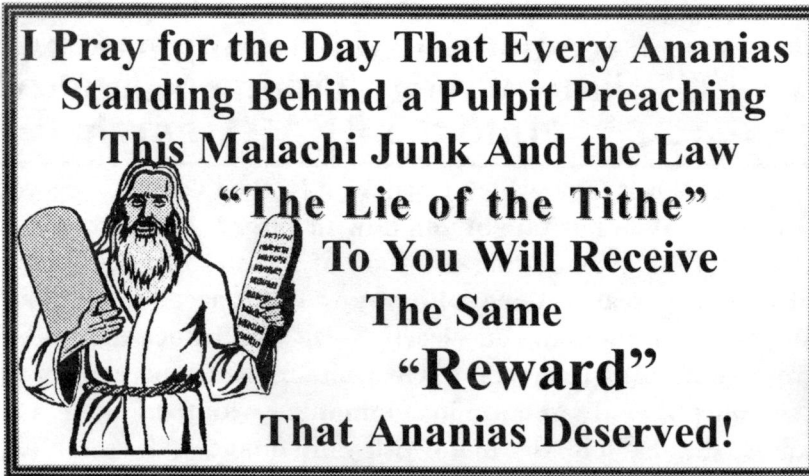

I Pray for the Day That Every Ananias Standing Behind a Pulpit Preaching This Malachi Junk And the Law "The Lie of the Tithe" To You Will Receive The Same "Reward" That Ananias Deserved!

Acts 11:27-29

27   And in these days prophets came from Jerusalem to Antioch.

28   Then one of them, named Agabus, stood up and showed by the Spirit that there was going to be a great famine throughout all the world, which also happened in the days of Claudius Caesar.

29 Then   the   disciples,   **EACH ACCORDING TO HIS ABILITY,** determined to send relief to the brethren dwelling in Judea. (NKJ)

If you read the Bible for only its "Word of God" content, you will miss a lot of history. There is a lot of history included within the confines of what you may call scripture. Here we find the prophet Agabus showing by the Power of the Spirit that a Great Famine was coming upon the world. History records that as famines go this was one of the worst. In fact, the situation got so bad during this time that reported <u>acts of human cannibalism</u> became quite common. Some historians recorded that in some instances **<u>mothers inside the gates of Jerusalem roasted and ate their own children</u>**. One of the greatest Ignorance's in Modern Christianity is its own ignorance by its members of what has happened historically. If there is one thing that God is, I can assure you, it is this … He Is the Only Author of History.

What is amazing about these passages apart from their historical merit can be seen in verse 29. You must realize that every disciple knew the <u>Very Serious and Destitute Situations</u> that many were facing in their day. Still, there was no <u>COMMAND</u> given to give your very best or to sacrificially give.

There was no mass appeal that you must help God out; just look at the suffering and give out of your own need at this time. They did not bring a large portfolio of pictures to look at the poor hungry faces of people throughout the land. This was not the time to start a world wide ministry to feed the poor.

It was a simple matter of helping your brother and sister out in a tough time, **IF YOU COULD.** There was no loud proclamation or shouting saying we are asking you to sacrifice at this time! No! A thousand times no! Under some of the most critical circumstances in all of history the disciples were asked only to ...

Give ... According to Your Ability! Do Not Give What You Do Not Have That You Become a Burden.

Today, we would have had camera crews with pictures of the destitute and probably a few mothers eating their babies for a total shock effect upon the viewer. There would have been immediate fund-raising efforts by ministries to help the poor. In reality, the only thing the disciples did was to give according to their ability. Give only if you have the ability to give. There was no condemnation or guilt inflicting words.

As I said, the situation that existed would be used by today's televangelists as a major fund-raising event. The disciples were only concerned with the BROTHERS AND SISTERS in Judea during this time. Somehow, I can hear the purveyors of the Gospel According to Mammon proclaiming, "some of you need to sacrifice as you have never sacrificed before."

It Would Absolutely Stun You ...
To see the Lifestyles of many Leaders Of ministries That are Involved In projecting the Destitute Images Of the Poor That you see on television

Simplicity says the disciples collected <u>ONLY</u> for <u>brothers</u> <u>and</u> <u>sisters</u>, with a simple request to give only what you have <u>according to your ability</u>. Do not give past your ability that you might become a burden yourself. My friend, if you cannot give, be free from the guilt and condemnation administered by many of today's hirelings. Remember, do not give what you do not have. Oh no, there goes putting your pledges on your charge card at 18 percent, Mr. Christian telethon. Wake up and grow up.

1 Cor 16:1-3

1 Now concerning <u>THE COLLECTION FOR THE SAINTS,</u> as I have given orders to the churches of Galatia, so you must do also:
2 On the first day of the week let each one of you lay something aside, <u>STORING UP AS HE MAY PROSPER</u>, that there be <u>NO COLLECTIONS</u> when I come.
3 And when I come, whomever you approve by your letters I will send to <u>BEAR YOUR GIFT TO JERUSALEM</u>.
(NKJ)

Here we can see another example of Paul collecting money <u>For The Poor Saints at Jerusalem</u>. You will notice in verse two that Paul <u>did not want</u> any collections taken up while he was there.

Well, there goes your typical love offering.

No one stood up and proclaimed!

"Well, you know what we need to do here, saints, is bless Brother Paul with a love offering." "Let's show Brother Paul just how much we appreciate his hard work and that good word he delivered to us tonight." Make you sick or what? I never allowed anyone to take a love offering for me because I had a feeling many times (because of my bold speaking), I was not loved too much. That did not matter. I am not for hire and you cannot hire me! Love offerings are just another way for your church hireling ... to pass on the expenses of another hireling to you while protecting their own funds. $ubtle schemes of men.

The important part of these passages is found in verse 2, where the people were told to lay something aside **ONLY** **AS** **THEY** **PROSPERED.** Isn't it ironic that so far in our last two passages we have found that <u>you are not to give what you do not have?</u> Here we are told to <u>give only on the increase,</u> as <u>you have prospered.</u>

It Is Clearly Evident That Paul Fully Understood That No One Had To Give and Especially If Your Life was In Need Itself! You would Have Been the Reason for The Gift!

Never, in the Entire Bible From Genesis to Revelations Will you find One Command To Ever Tithe or Give While Life Is on the Decreasing Scale.

The silver tongued televangelists of our day have made merchandise of thousands of innocent souls, twisting the scriptures for their own benefit and destruction, to whom outer darkness and the judgment of the Lord awaits them. The Lord is coming and his face is full of fury against those who Prostitute the Gospel for a Buck and count The Blood of the Covenant an Unholy thing! Take heart, my friend, the Lord does not sleep and He is not slack concerning those who Masquerade as Angels of Light in rewarding those of this generation who have grown to a Full Manifestation of Evil.

Rejoice ... the darkness of our day will bring about another climax in the History of God. We are on the verge of a genuine move by God to bring Restoration and Reality to the Body of Christ. **Many will perish, many hearts will fail, real faith will be hard to find, but "from the rubble," Reality Will Arise!**

In the early '90s, I was having meetings in my home on Friday nights. A young girl sat on my couch with a perplexed look on her face. She had just listened to part one of my teachings on the Lie of Tithing. She said to me, "I don't know what to do because by the time I pay my tithes I never have enough money to buy food. Many times I go without food and I do not understand why it is taking God so long to bless me. He must be really testing my faith." I literally thought my neck and head would explode right off my body. This young girl attended a church called the Sanctuary in Deland, Florida. It was anything **BUT** a sanctuary.

It was over run with spiders, witches, and warlocks. The pastor at that time was Michael Coleman, an End Times Escapism Lunatic. You will never know how badly I wanted to wake Michael Coleman up that night. A few years later, Mike and I would have several confrontations, which are mentioned in the book, "Christianity a Hoax?" I Spoke directly To Mike over the Radio and told him that God would Take His Heart out of "Ministry." Mike is no longer at the Sanctuary and is running around trying to keep something going. Thank You Lord for removing the heart of another Heretic!

Patiently, I explained the following to this young girl. I hope this example will help you if you have ever been trapped by the craftiness of man as she was. I asked her to imagine with me for a moment that she had children. Her children had borrowed some money from her agreeing to pay it back at the rate of one hundred dollars per month. They did okay for a while but then they started skipping payments. I asked her if she went to her children's home to collect her payment and found that they had no money, food, and their water and electricity had been cut off, would she demand her hundred dollar payment?

"Why no," she replied. "I am not that heartless."

To which I responded, "Then, why do you think that your Father in heaven has a heart smaller than yours? He is not interested in how much you put in the basket when you are hungry YOURSELF. Your Father's heart is full when He knows you are eating as He has provided for you; just as yours would be knowing that your children and grandchildren had food." God receives NO GLORY from these foolish acts of self-debasing commitment by you. Show me this behavior in the Bible. REMEMBER THESE TWO THINGS: DO NOT GIVE WHAT YOU DO NOT HAVE THAT YOU MAY BECOME A BURDEN AND GIVE ONLY AS YOU HAVE PROSPERED.

2 Cor 8:1-15

1   Moreover, brethren, we make known to you the grace of God bestowed on the churches of Macedonia:

2   that in a great trial of affliction the abundance of their joy and their deep poverty abounded in the riches of their liberality.

3   For I bear witness that according to their ability, yes, and beyond their ability, they were <u>freely willing,</u>

4   imploring us with much urgency that we would receive the gift and the fellowship of the ministering to the saints.

5   And not only as we had hoped, but they first gave themselves to the Lord, and then to us by the will of God.

6   So we urged Titus, that as he had begun, so he would also complete this grace in you as well.

7   But as you abound in everything-- in faith, in speech, in knowledge, in all diligence, and in your love for us-- see that you abound in this grace also.

8   I <u>SPEAK</u> <u>NOT</u> <u>BY</u> <u>COMMANDMENT,</u> but I am testing the sincerity of your love by the diligence of others.

9   For you know the grace of our Lord Jesus Christ, that though He was rich, yet for your sakes He became poor, that you through His poverty might become rich.

10   And in this I give advice: It is to your advantage not only to be doing what you began and were desiring to do a year ago;

11   but now you also must complete the doing of it; that as there was a readiness to desire it, so there also may be a completion out of what you have.

12   <u>FOR</u> <u>IF</u> <u>THERE</u> <u>IS</u> <u>FIRST</u> <u>A</u> <u>WILLING</u> <u>MIND,</u> <u>IT</u> <u>IS</u> <u>ACCEPTED</u> <u>ACCORDING</u> <u>TO</u> <u>WHAT</u> <u>ONE</u> <u>HAS,</u> <u>AND</u> <u>NOT</u> <u>ACCORDING</u> <u>TO</u> <u>WHAT</u> <u>HE</u> <u>DOES</u> <u>NOT</u> <u>HAVE.</u>

13   <u>FOR</u> <u>I</u> <u>DO</u> <u>NOT</u> <u>MEAN</u> <u>THAT</u> <u>OTHERS</u> <u>SHOULD</u> <u>BE</u> <u>EASED</u> <u>AND</u> <u>YOU</u> <u>BURDENED;</u>

14   but by an equality, that now at this time your abundance may supply their lack, that their abundance also may supply your lack-- that there may be equality.

15   As it is written, "He who gathered much had nothing left over, and he who gathered little had no lack." (NKJ)

In Chapter 8 we find Paul beginning with a strong admonishment to the Corinthians church over a gift they had promised to send to the poor saints. He begins by using the church in Macedonia as an example. He explains that in a great trial of affliction and deep poverty that they took up this fellowship of ministering to the saints. <u>Remember, the collection was for the poor saints in Jerusalem and Judea who were in the midst of one of the greatest famines that ever hit the planet.</u> Paul encourages the Corinthians church in verse 7 to see that they abound in this type of grace since they had said they were going to do it. However, he qualifies it by saying, "<u>I</u> <u>speak</u> not <u>by</u> <u>Commandment</u>." According to vs. 10 and 11 they had been in the process of getting the money together for some time; over a year evidently, and he was encouraging them to complete what they had offered to do.

Remember, the collection was for the saints! Money in the entire New Testament was collected <u>FOR NO OTHER REASON</u>. The entire focus of Chapter 8 comes down to vs. 11 through 15 as Paul begins to explain how this completion was to be accomplished in verse 11. It must be done <u>ONLY</u> out of <u>What</u> <u>You</u> <u>Have</u>.

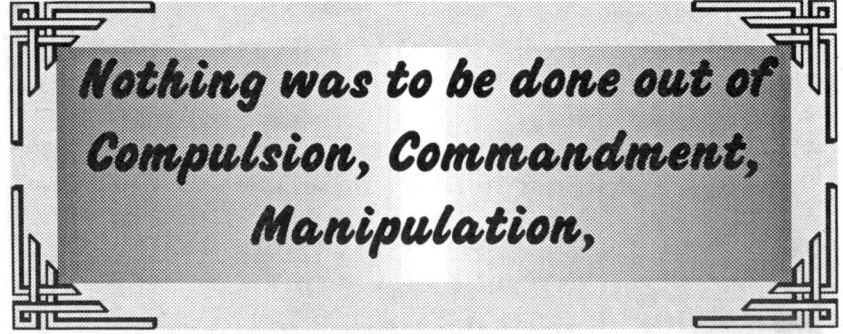

Nothing was to be done out of Compulsion, Commandment, Manipulation,

PAUL GOES ON TO SAY IN VERSE 12

That everything is Acceptable <u>Only</u> According to what you have and Not According to what you <u>DO NOT</u> have.

The Grace of that statement was intended to take all of the burden off of the backs of those who did not have. It carries the same implications for you. He clearly explains once again in verse 13 that it does absolutely no good for anyone to give to someone else in order for their burden to be eased, and that you become a burden yourself. What good is that?

In verses 14 and 15,

If you will Look and Study, You will find one of the Most Powerful Statements On

REAL FAITH

In All of Scripture.

14   but by an equality, that now at this time your abundance may supply their lack, that their abundance also may supply your lack-- that there may be equality.
15   As it is written, "He who gathered much had nothing left over, and he who gathered little had no lack." (NKJ)

What Paul was basically saying is this: Saints, the Essence of living by Faith is SEEING a need and meeting it According to Your Ability. So that your life exists with nothing left over, it does not matter if you gather much, or if you have little; the Love of your brother would take away your lack in your time of need.

You will not find barns or storehouses anywhere in the Kingdom of Christ! Your hand should never be empty or full. It sounds like to me that Paul was preaching "Childlike Faith," total dependence on God as your Sovereign Source.

When you were a child, how often did you go to sleep wondering how you were going to make the mortgage payment? Were you concerned that the light or water bill may be higher than expected? Did you lay in bed and worry about your job or boss problems? Jesus said, "Lest you become as a little child you shall not inherit the Kingdom of God." What has happened to you that you cannot relate to God your Father as a Child? All I worried about as a Little Child was Play. What about YOU? What did you worry about? Isn't it time you became as a Little Child Again?

The New Testament is full of the Apostle Paul's continuous Fight Against the Physical Act of Circumcision. Why would Paul get all shook up over a little Piece of Foreskin? With this one Physical act Paul Destroys All Of the LAW. Tithing was not the Issue In those days because everyone ATE THE TITHE. A good study to research is all of the Apostle Paul's arguments against the act of Physical Circumcision.

Beleive me, if Paul were here today
He would Fight the Physical Circumcision
Of your Wallet!

Paul, again in these passages, issues another caution **against giving what you do not have.** I can assure you that every time you have done that the tools of Condemnation, Guilt, and Control were used on you by a Master Manipulator. In addition, if you will check your heart, you will discover that possibly there was a spirit of pride living within your heart that provoked you to do more than you should.

I would do you a disservice if I let them get away with the statements of how Jesus became poor so that you might become rich in verse 9. If that interpretation is to mean literal physical riches, then we must throw everything else away and the entire Chapter 8 will have to be declared as completely out of balance with verse nine. If you have not caught on yet, Tithing within Christianity is <u>NOT</u> about money. This Gospel is about Spiritual Riches and Our Inheritance of those riches in Christ alone.

Jesus gave many examples using physical substances
TO TEACH US A SPIRITUAL LESSON.

He never taught anyone how to make money, or that any act of His would result in physical riches becoming your inheritance.

For anyone to teach Monetary Gain in the name of Christ is blasphemous and heresy of the highest kind. I have met people with a Mercedes sticker pinned to their blouse walking around like an idiot claiming and confessing that God was going to give them one. We can thank Kenneth Copland, Kenneth Hagin, Oral Roberts, Fred Price, Creflo Dollar, and every other prosperity lunatic for birthing such foolishness.

Our entire study is to gain the Spiritual Understanding of Why, for What reason, and for Who money was collected in the New Testament church.

In our examination of the New Testament Epistles we are searching for Proof that the Law of Tithing was Abolished in Christ. If we cannot find anywhere in the Entire New Testament where a Tithe was collected for any other reason than the saints, then we must conclude that Tithing was Not a New Testament practice.

You should really begin to think about the glorious building programs by Churches built for a one hour service. In this Generation of "<u>Let Me Entertain You Christianity</u>," <u>YOU will have to decide to walk away from THE ILLUSION or you will NEVER find Reality!</u>

2 Cor 9:5-13

5   Therefore I thought it necessary to exhort the brethren to go to you ahead of time, and prepare your generous gift beforehand, which you had previously promised, that it may be ready <u>as a matter of generosity and not as a grudging obligation.</u>

6   But this I say: He who sows sparingly will also reap sparingly, and he who sows bountifully will also reap bountifully.

7   <u>So let each one give as he purposes in his heart, not grudgingly or of necessity;</u> for God loves a cheerful giver.

8   And God is able to make all grace abound toward you, that you, always having all sufficiency in all things, may have an abundance for every good work.

9   As it is written: "He has dispersed abroad, he has given to the poor; his righteousness endures forever."

10   Now may He who supplies seed to the sower, and bread for food, supply and multiply the seed you have sown and increase the fruits of your righteousness,

11   while you are enriched in everything for all liberality, which causes thanksgiving through us to God.

12   For the administration of this service not only supplies the needs of the saints, but also is abounding through many thanksgivings to God,

13   while, through the proof of this ministry, they glorify God for the obedience of your confession to the gospel of Christ, and for your liberal sharing with them and all men,(NKJ)

Here we find Paul once again exhorting the Corinthians to complete their free will offering to send relief to the saints. Paul makes it very clear in verse 5 that the entire matter is one of their own generosities and not one of obligation. This is very important in understanding what he means in the following verse 6 where he speaks about sowing and reaping bountifully or sparingly. The entire issue of sowing and reaping spoke about a heart issue. This is especially clear if you compare what we looked at in Chapter 8. I do not think it is wise to study these two Chapters separately, since they both are connected and written in the same thought pattern.

Paul makes it clear
That everything given
Should be from the heart.
A Heart Free from the <u>Law,</u>
<u>Bondage,</u> <u>Compulsion,</u> <u>or</u>
<u>Grudging</u> <u>Stinginess.</u>
The Gift should be a Matter of
Generosity
Found Within the Heart.

If <u>you</u> <u>cannot</u> <u>find</u> <u>that</u> <u>within</u> <u>your</u> <u>heart,</u> <u>then</u> <u>do</u> <u>not</u> <u>give</u> <u>what</u> <u>you</u> <u>do</u> <u>not</u> <u>have</u> <u>or</u> <u>give</u> <u>out</u> <u>of</u> <u>necessity.</u> The heart should also be void of any grudging or feelings of obligation. Paul says you were <u>**NOT TO GIVE**</u> out of necessity. Oops, there goes your giving to get gospel and greedy mentality. He clearly points out that everything was to be done only as an Individual Purposed in <u>His</u> Heart. The entire issue of sowing and reaping bountifully or sparingly was used to point out a heart condition. Anytime you give and you find it a burden, <u>YOU</u> have a heart problem. Stingy hearts will always begrudge anything. Paul makes it clear that God loves a cheerful giver, one without any stingy attitudes or giving to get greedy ways. Sowing and Reaping "Natural" Theology Is Rooted In one thing ... GREED!

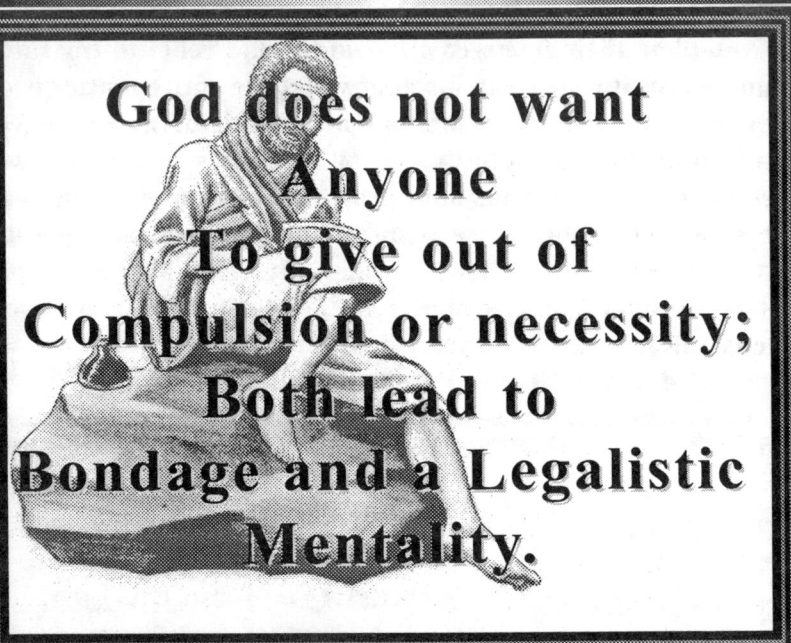

**God does not want
Anyone
To give out of
Compulsion or necessity;
Both lead to
Bondage and a Legalistic
Mentality.**

This is the Same Principle we found in the Old Testament. Free Will offerings were just that, Your own free Will. The fastest way to mess up a Pure Heart is to force it to do something it does not want to do! Who wants a relationship with anyone that would force you to go against your Heart?

Paul continues to emphasize this in verse 10 by pointing out that everything in our life comes from God who <u>supplies both seed and bread to us for the purpose of increasing our righteousness.</u> It is amazing to me how many people can remain closed fisted and stingy. It all comes down to the realization that Everything in Your Life and All Sufficiency comes from God. What He looks for is the condition of your heart and how well it relates to the needs of others. He never wants you to do anything above or beyond what you have. When you try to do that you leave Grace and Enter Works and Law.

To your Father, it is a matter of doing with what you have right where you are. It will require you to be in total dependence, living by faith at the hand of God, just like a Child. <u>Sound familiar; why do you find this so difficult?</u>

The reason the gospel of giving to get sells so well is because they know the greedy imperfections that live within the chambers of your heart. This is why it is so critical to your own faith that you finally enter a Real Personal Relationship with your Father and your finances. When you realize it is your heart that He desires, and His only desire is to build a heart that will be Profitable for the Kingdom family business. It will go well with you!

We can see also in these passages that there was much praise and glory given to the Father throughout the land. The Father was Glorified because of the loving kindness expressed through the lives of His children. This principle of the Father receiving Glory unto Himself has been a Predominant Principle in <u>every</u> <u>aspect</u> of our study of tithing and giving by His children. One of the hardest things you will ever do is become honest with yourself and admit you cannot hear him in the Carnal Realm of Money. <u>When you get there, you are on your way!</u> The next step will be to allow Him to express Himself to, in, and through your life. <u>What a journey!</u> Think about it; you can trade Religion for Reality. Haven't you carried the burden of the law long enough?

Be free ...

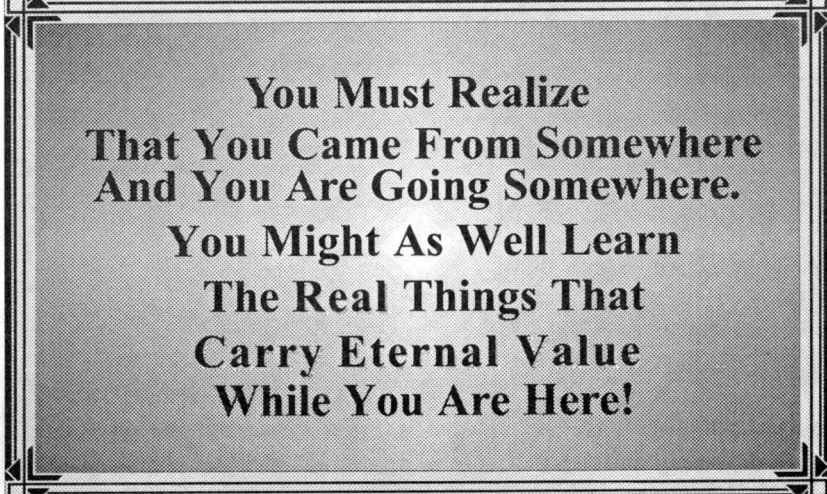

**You Must Realize
That You Came From Somewhere
And You Are Going Somewhere.
You Might As Well Learn
The Real Things That
Carry Eternal Value
While You Are Here!**

Hebrews Chapter 7:1-22
READ ... READ ... READ!
It's about a Priesthood
Not a Tithe!

1   For this Melchizedek, king of Salem, priest of the Most High God, who met Abraham returning from the slaughter of the kings and blessed him,

2   to whom also Abraham gave a tenth part of all, first being translated "king of righteousness," and then also king of Salem, meaning "king of peace,"

3   without father, without mother, without genealogy, having neither beginning of days nor end of life, but made like the Son of God, remains a priest continually.

4   Now consider how great this man was, to whom even the patriarch Abraham gave a tenth of the spoils.

5   And indeed those who are of the sons of Levi, who receive the priesthood, have a commandment to receive tithes from the people according to the law, that is, from their brethren, though they have come from the loins of Abraham;

6   but he whose genealogy is not derived from them received tithes from Abraham and blessed him who had the promises.

7   Now beyond all contradiction the lesser is blessed by the better.

8   HERE MORTAL MEN RECEIVE TITHES, BUT THERE HE RECEIVES THEM, OF WHOM IT IS WITNESSED THAT HE LIVES.

9   Even Levi, who receives tithes, PAID TITHES THROUGH Abraham, so to speak,

10   for he was still in the loins of his father when Melchizedek met him.

READ READ

11   THEREFORE, IF PERFECTION WERE THROUGH THE LEVITICAL PRIESTHOOD (FOR UNDER IT THE PEOPLE RECEIVED THE LAW), WHAT FURTHER NEED WAS THERE THAT ANOTHER PRIEST SHOULD RISE ACCORDING TO THE ORDER OF MELCHIZEDEK, AND NOT BE CALLED ACCORDING TO THE ORDER OF AARON?

12   For the priesthood being changed, of necessity there is also a change of the law.

13   For He of whom these things are spoken belongs to another tribe, from which no man has officiated at the altar.

14   For it is evident that our Lord arose from Judah, of which tribe Moses spoke nothing concerning priesthood.

15   And it is yet far more evident if, in the likeness of Melchizedek, there arises another priest

16   who has come, not according to the law of a fleshly commandment, but according to the power of an endless life.

17   For He testifies: "You are a priest forever according to the order of Melchizedek."

18   For on the one hand there is an annulling of the former commandment because of its weakness and unprofitableness,

19   FOR THE LAW MADE NOTHING PERFECT; on the other hand, there is the bringing in of a better hope, through which we draw near to God.

20   And inasmuch as He was not made priest without an oath

21   (for they have become priests without an oath, but He with an oath by Him who said to Him: "THE LORD HAS SWORN AND WILL NOT RELENT, 'YOU ARE A PRIEST FOREVER ACCORDING TO THE ORDER OF MELCHIZEDEK' "),

22   BY SO MUCH MORE Jesus has become a surety of a better covenant. (NKJ)

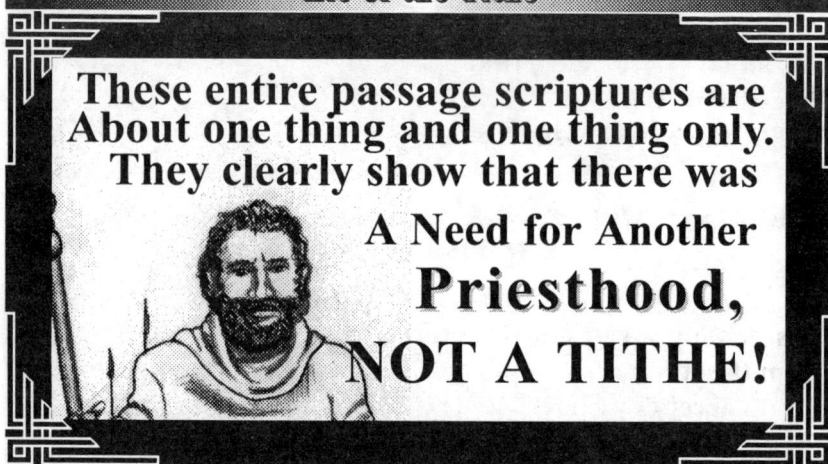

These entire passage scriptures are About one thing and one thing only. They clearly show that there was

A Need for Another

Priesthood,

NOT A TITHE!

EVERY PASSAGE OF SCRIPTURE IS ABOUT ABRAHAM SIGNIFYING THAT THERE WOULD ONE DAY BE A PRIESTHOOD THAT WOULD NOT HAVE EARTHLY LINEAGE.

In all of the Old Testament, even a casual observer can see that family lineage and genealogy was a very important issue. You know the parts that say so and so begat so and so. The significance of this is highly relevant to this priest Melchizedek, a priest without mother or father and without any lineage to any tribe. The writer clearly makes his point in verse 11 that if perfection came through the Levitical priesthood there would not have been a need for another.

This entire Chapter validates everything I taught in the Genesis encounter between Abraham and Melchizedek. I have underlined many passages in this Chapter for your benefit. Please take the time to read them and impart truth within your heart. Abraham gave Melchizedek a portion of the spoils of war; he did not give him anything of his own. In our study in Genesis, Abraham clearly testified that it was God who had given him the victory.

Remember Abraham declared to the king of Sodom and Gomorrah that he had lifted his hand to God saying ... that he would take nothing "not even a shoelace." If you are still somewhat confused about Abraham and Melchizedek, I suggest that you reread the account in Genesis again.

The scriptures are so clear about the Father of Faith Abraham signifying that there would one day come a Priesthood Without Mother or Father or Earthly Lineage. Unlike the Levitical priesthood that would not accept anything that had the slightest flaw of imperfections anywhere, this priesthood Melchizedek would accept tithes from the spoils of a war.

Abraham, signifying by his acts of faith, showed that this coming priesthood could be offered nothing that came from the strength of man's own hand. This coming priesthood would accept imperfections! It is important to remember that the Tithes from the Spoils of War given to Melchizedek by Abraham signified that this Priesthood would accept nothing by man's own hand.

A Priest Forever After The Order Of Melchizedek!

The Priesthood That was to Come Would also Take Filthy Tithes.

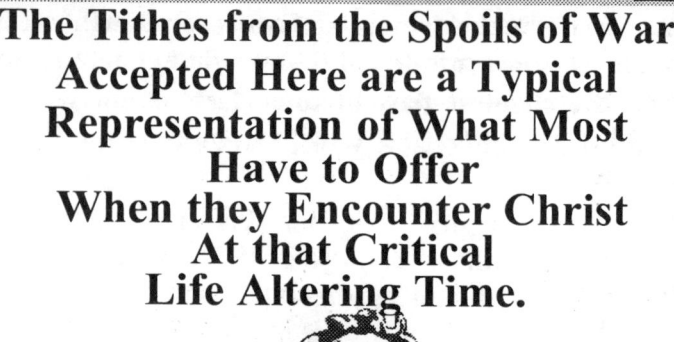

The Tithes from the Spoils of War
Accepted Here are a Typical
Representation of What Most
Have to Offer
When they Encounter Christ
At that Critical
Life Altering Time.

Nothing!

Nothing but the Leftover
"Spoils Of a War Torn Life"
Ravaged By Decadence and Sin.

The importance of spiritually realizing that Abraham's ability to give tithes from the spoils of war that came from God is crucial. Abraham clearly proclaimed that it was God who had given him the victory and that nothing came by the strength of his own hand. The Spiritual Significance of this gives Credibility to the Entire Born Again Experience. God the Father orchestrates the entire matter; and there is nothing you can offer Him at that critical time, <u>except the spoils from a ravaged war torn sinful life.</u>

The next time you hear a preacher say Abraham paid tithes and so should you, he is Carnal within his heart. His eyes can only see the natural; his heart has been trained on covetous practices. This man never fulfilled the first requirement of all ministry; he never overcame the Power of Mammon! From the outset of his ministry he was still in bondage to Mammon and never came to know Christ Intimately enough to know Him as the Sovereign source of all things. Whatever ministry God may have entrusted to this man stands in the Power of His Own Flesh. This man will build anything and everything in the name of God using the Law of Tithing. He comes fully equipped with the tools of bondage, condemnation, and guilt with one purpose. To Manipulate the Children of God!

Think with me for a moment. Sit on the Pew and Here Comes the Plate ... What are your Real Feelings? How Do you feel when you put nothing in the basket? Have you ever acted like you put something in? Do you feel like people are watching you? Even if you put something in on Sunday Morning, how did you feel on Sunday night when the basket came by again? Why do they Take so many Collections? If God is talking to you ... He is the one that Makes You Feel Uncomfortable when the Plate comes your way. God is the one that makes you aware of the eyes of the Usher. If this is you ... Rejoice! If, on the other hand, you are the one that continues in your pride to practice Religion. If you like the Plate or Basket and you feel nothing ... God is not speaking to you. However take heart ... He will one day ... He will say to all of the Goats ...

"DEPART FROM ME!"

Driven by their egos, most Cheerleaders will create lots of programs, many useless activities, useless gatherings, along with tons of religious works. He will also include you in visitation, Wednesday night service, cell groups, home meetings, building fund-raisers, car washes, bake sales, garage sales, Sunday school, Bible studies, leadership training, sisters of the light, and brothers of the night. All of these activities will never introduce you to the Deep Realities of knowing Christ and allowing him true Lordship over your life.

I remember sitting in class one day while I was attending ministry school in Euless, Texas. The teacher that day was Pastor Doug White of Restoration Church. Doug was an excellent teacher and seemed to be well liked and respected by many. I believe he was teaching a class on how to study the Bible when I heard him say, "Abraham paid tithes and so should you." It was at that point that he seemed to go on a small rampage about tithing. By the time he was finished, I am sure everyone felt the sting of Doug's Guilt, Condemnation, and Pastoral Manipulation.

Years later I would send Pastor Doug a two-hour teaching video on "The Lie of the Tithe" with an open challenge to prove it wrong. I figured that Doug White had enough integrity as a man to admit error if he was wrong. I was wrong about Doug. I also assumed that since he taught the class on how to study the Bible he would at least put good biblical hermeneutics to practice and search the matter out. It is over 10 years and Doug is still unable to take the tithing challenge or prove it wrong. How sad for those who sit under him.

Let's Put Three Nails In It!

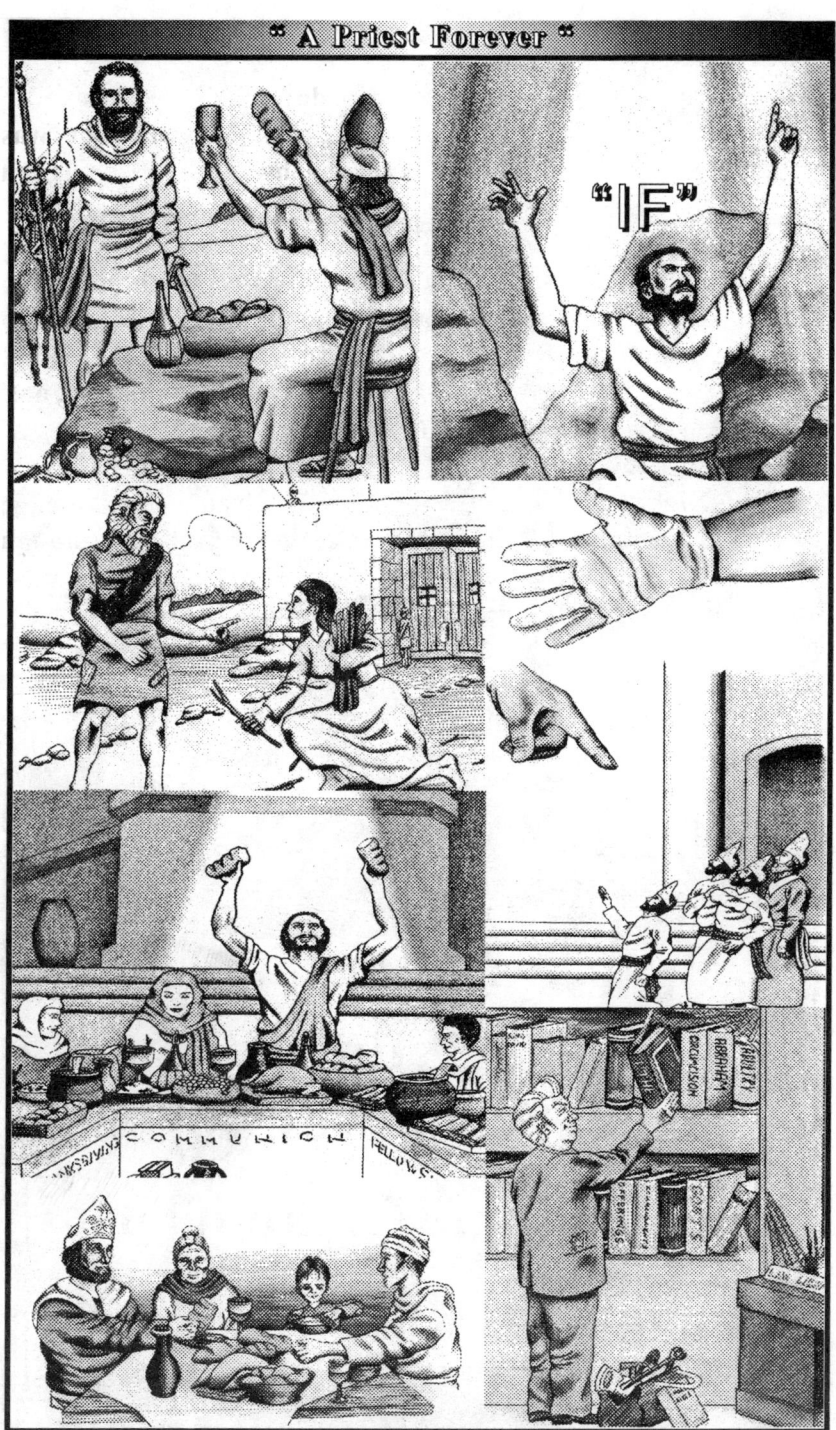

It Is Finished!

Saints, I hope you have enjoyed our study. With my Whole Heart, I Urge You to seriously consider the Grave Consequences, as well as, the Extreme Grace found in Paul's Last Words To the New Church.

These Are Absolutely The Most Important Scriptures.

Read Them...CommitThem
To Memory!

Gal 3:10-13
A Curse ... And Grace

10 For as many as are of the works of the law are under the curse; for it is written, "Cursed is everyone who does not continue in all things which are written in the book of the law, to do them."

11 But that no one is justified by the law in the sight of God is evident, for "the just shall live by faith."

12 Yet the law is not of faith, but "the man who does them shall live by them."

Paul Makes It Very Clear In Verse 10 That Anyone Who Works In The Law Is Working In A Curse. Is That You? The Law Is Not Of Faith!

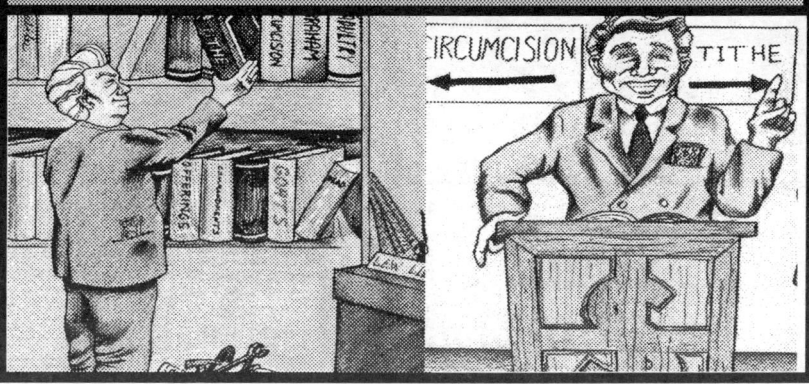

Galations 3:13

13 <u>Christ has redeemed **US**</u>

<u>from the curse of the law,</u>

<u>**having become**</u>

<u>**a curse for us**</u>

<u>(for it is written,</u>
<u>"Cursed is everyone who hangs</u>
<u>on a tree").</u>

Think with me for a moment, please.
<u>Since Christ became a Curse for **US**</u>
In order to Redeem **US**
From the Curse of the Law;
Then what are <u>**YOU**</u> doing
Dabbling in a Curse?

Think about how Offensive it must be to God, For you as a Redeemed Son or Daughter of God, To be <u>Dabbling in the Bondage</u> of a Curse.

Since God allowed Christ to become a curse for US because of the Law why would you practice the "LIE OF THE TITHE?" <u>Why would you desecrate the Sacrifice of Christ and call God's Plan Incomplete by your Actions?</u> As Paul said, "for it is written, cursed is everyone who hangs on a tree." Then why would you pick up the curse of the law and play with it? **<u>For as many as are under the law are under a curse:</u>** "Cursed is everyone who <u>DOES NOT CONTINUE</u> in <u>All</u> things which are written in the book of the Law to do them."

When You Practice "The Lie of the Tithe" You are working in a Curse!

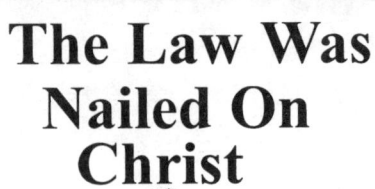

**If you are a legalistic tither,
You violate the Grace of God.
Your every action calls
The completed work of the Cross
To be null and void,
A useless thing.**

You do not have to tithe 10 percent to be a legalistic tither. In fact, you probably try to stay close to 10 percent but you will find yourself going over and under that depending on your financial situation over time. You will also live with a constant mental account of how much you owe God, making sure that your account is always paid up. God forbid, you would die and owe God money! You think that when you get to heaven God is going to give you a Good Tither Badge. There are none!

Everyone likes to think that they are God's little helper on the earth. Legalistic Tithers like to think that their money helped God keep His church going.

**Pure Law is the Shroud
Upon your Heart.**

Somehow, within your heart, God might not have been able to do it without your help. You have been deceived; you have been robbed of a real relationship with God based on one thing, Faith alone and the total redemptive work of the cross.

**It is <u>Extremely Offensive</u>
To your Father
For you to take the
Totality of His Grace
And to pick up the law
Declaring that the works of
<u>Your Hands</u> are Better than
Christ's <u>Finished</u> Work at Calvary.**

Let's face it. Tithing has always been about communion with the Father. It started in the Old Testament where the tither would come and have a meal with the Father to the New Testament where that communion is now by Faith in Christ alone. Just as the Old Testament tither was to symbolically eat his meal in the presence of the Father, so have you been called to that Spiritual Communion with Christ.

Can You Hear Him?

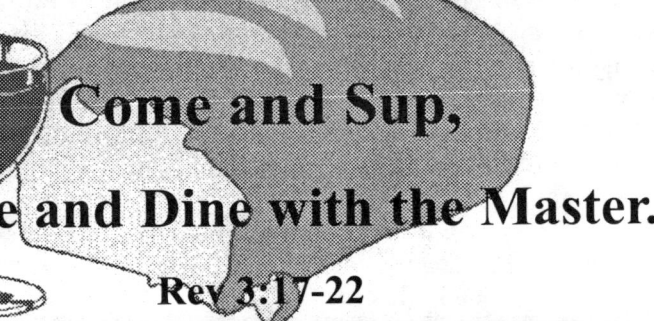

Come and Sup,

Come and Dine with the Master.

Rev 3:17-22

"Because you say, 'I am rich, have become wealthy, and have need of nothing'-- and do not know that you are wretched, miserable, poor, blind, and naked--

"I counsel you to buy from Me gold refined in the fire, that you may be rich; and white garments, that you may be clothed, that the shame of your nakedness may not be revealed; and anoint your eyes with eye salve, that you may see.

"As many as I love, I rebuke and chasten. Therefore be zealous and repent.

"Behold, I stand at the door and knock. If anyone <u>HEARS</u> My voice and opens the door ...

<u>I will</u>
<u>Come in to him and dine with him,</u>
<u>And he with Me.</u>

My Prayer for You

May it be so for you, may you be delivered from the Bondage of the Law. May you find Reality, Communion, and Fellowship with the Father. May your heart be healed from the wounds inflicted by the Religious Charlatans of our day. Let the chains of Bondage, Guilt, Manipulation, and Control be Broken from your Life.

Walk in Grace apart from the Law, purpose in your heart to know God while you are here. <u>Do not Give Another Dime</u> to a Reprobate Man Made Religious Institution. Learn to hear God for yourself! Allow Him to build in and through you what He wants. Know the joy of Touching a Life as a Vessel of God.

May you inherit a Bold Heart to stand in this Desperate Generation. May the Father impart to you A Voice that carries the sound of a Pure Trumpet proclaiming ... This is the Way ...

May your life be a living Demonstration to those in need around you that you have the One True God. Bend the knee and the heart! Allow the Father to Extract Glory from your Life unto Himself!

ABOVE ALL BE FREE!

Special Thanks to Artist Jerome Tso for his diligent Effort in helping to Communicate a Difficult Subject. Jerome may be contacted directly at P.O. Box 14 Chinle Az. 86503

Videos

"The Lie of The Tithe" ... The original teaching nearly Two Hours of nonstop insight. If you enjoyed the book you will not believe the video ... $19.95

"Politics or Christ" .... If you are a political Christian, you must see this! You will never forget the undeniable Truths contained on this one! The content is wide-open revelation of the Christian Political Movement. Find out what scripture really says about Christian Politics ... $19.95

"Lordship" ... The Absolute Must Watch Video Series! For Serious Truth Seekers Only! Guaranteed to profoundly impact your Life or a full refund is yours! Titles are ... Chasing Straw ... Motive ... Is there A Man of God in the City ... Faith that Crosses Lines ... Beyond the Lines Tapes are $19.95 ea. or the Entire Series for $79.00

"Benny Hinn Conspiracy" ... Actual News Reports of Benny's Conspiracy with The Orange County Sheriff's Office! You will not believe what Benny is up to ... Benny Paid Off Nine Judas' to Silence the Matter. This is one HOT tape that Benny hopes you never see! Included in the Tape are the Names of the Nine Judas' who betrayed Christ for a Dollar! One may live near you. Remember this ... Innocent People Do Not Pay!
Must See $12.95

For a complete list of over 50 tapes and books visit our Web Site on the Internet at SimpleTruths.net

*** All books and tapes add $5.00 S/H ***